D0482976

ETSY EXCELLENCE

DID YOU KNOW?

»→ TODAY ON ETSY, MORE THAN 1 MILLION SELLERS
ARE CONNECTING WITH SOME 20 MILLION BUYERS

»→ ALMOST HALF A MILLION ETSY SELLERS ARE EARN-
ING A LIVING EXCLUSIVELY FROM THEIR ETSY SHOPS

»→ 75 PERCENT OF ETSY SELLERS SEE THEIR SHOPS
AS VIABLE SMALL BUSINESSES

»→ 33 PERCENT OF ETSY SELLERS DESCRIBE THEIR
SOLE OCCUPATION AS RUNNING THEIR ETSY SHOPS

»→ THE MOST SUCCESSFUL HANDMADE GOODS
SHOP ON ETSY EARNS $65,000 A MONTH

ETSY EXCELLENCE

THE SIMPLE GUIDE TO CREATING
A THRIVING ETSY BUSINESS

TYCHO
PRESS

CONTENTS

E tsy is a vibrant, innovative community where artists, crafters, and collectors use cutting-edge technology to sell their products—and in the process, many sellers have become business mavens in record time. On Etsy, rare antiques shine next to original fine art and quirky handmade jewelry, and the whole enterprise crosses boundaries of language and currency while maintaining a spirit of informality and fun.

But don't be fooled by that down-home vibe. Etsy is a thriving marketplace where billions of dollars change hands every year, and where a minimal investment can produce monumental results.

Whether you've just opened your first Etsy shop or have been an Etsy seller for years, this book will give you insider secrets and proven strategies for retaining loyal customers and increasing sales.

What can you do to make a splash in the Etsy pool? How can you create a presence and transform your products into cash on a regular basis? How can you elevate your brand, surpass your current potential, and claim your place on Etsy?

You can begin by understanding that elevating your brand means thriving on Etsy, not just surviving. And before you can thrive, you need amazing products and outstanding customer service. What are the keys to running a successful Etsy shop, one where high-quality products combine with attentive customer service to create a sustainable, profitable business?

- INNOVATION. Innovate by creating unique products that make a positive contribution to the existing marketplace.
- RELEVANCE. Stay relevant by writing product descriptions that make prospective buyers feel they've not only found what they were looking for but also discovered something they can no longer live without.
- PRESENTATION. Present your products in a professional way by using high-quality photographs.
- EFFICIENCY. When you're efficient in production and customer service, you create a sustainable, profitable business.
- VISIBILITY. Become visible as an Etsy seller by increasing your ability to show up prominently in potential customers' search results, by becoming a contributing member of the Etsy community, and by consistently making your shop attractive to qualified traffic (an e-commerce term referring to shop visitors who are ready to buy).

It's a steep learning curve, but you're in good company, as you'll see when you read the comments and advice culled from interviews with hundreds of experienced Etsy sellers. It is possible for your Etsy shop to stand out. It is possible for you to build a brand as reputable as that of a traditional brick-and-mortar store. It is possible for you to make good money online. You just need to be willing to do the work and use the strategies described in this book.

PART

1

KNOW WHAT ETSY CAN (AND CAN'T) DO FOR YOU

You've paid your 20-cent start-up fee, handcrafted a labor-of-love inventory, dreamed up the best shop name ever, and opened your digital doors. Now, besides talent and excitement, what will it take for you to stand out and make an impact as an Etsy seller? How can you make this marriage of art and e-commerce last forever? More important, how can you make Etsy work for you? Etsy offers many channels for streamlining your success, and taking advantage of its support will benefit you and your customers.

This part of the book focuses on the possibilities and challenges of being an Etsy seller, how to set goals for your Etsy shop, and learning from the early mistakes of seasoned Etsy shop owners.

UNDERSTANDING POSSIBILITIES AND AVOIDING PITFALLS

This book makes three basic assumptions:

1. You have a compelling product that you believe in.
2. Creating an Etsy shop will be a sound business decision for you.
3. You're willing to put in the effort it takes to learn the business side of things or take your current marketing skills to the next level.

SEIZE YOUR OPPORTUNITY

Etsy has made the commitment to serve online shoppers who have a desire in mind, a need to fill, and disposable cash in hand that they are ready to spend. In other words, Etsy is committed to serving the qualified traffic that the site is designed to bring to sellers' online shops.

Etsy is equally committed to celebrating and serving the creative independent entrepreneurs who are the company's lifeblood. As you gain insider knowledge and learn from other sellers' innovative marketing strategies, you'll be setting yourself up for the success that Etsy wants you to have. And as soon as you open an Etsy shop, you're automatically affiliated with a respected brand. Customers are familiar with Etsy, and familiarity in this case breeds comfort, confidence, assumptions of reliability and professionalism, and trust in the security of financial transactions.

As a company, Etsy is highly motivated to help your shop succeed. Why? Part of the answer lies in Etsy's commitment to the independent entrepreneurial spirit—but an even bigger part is the fact that Etsy earns 3.5 percent of every sale on the site, so your success directly affects the company's bottom line. Learn the lay of Etsyland, and your shop's success won't be far behind.

REACH FOR A HELPING HAND

Although Etsy offers sellers great opportunities and strong support, you may face real challenges. For example, Etsy sellers have expressed frustration about the likelihood of even being noticed among so many other Etsy shops, the difficulty of keeping the right number of items in stock, the obstacles to landing a click-through sale, and what some perceive as the predominantly female-oriented tone of the site. These are all valid issues, and it's important not to dismiss them. Here are some of the people, processes, platforms, and programs Etsy's most successful sellers have learned to use and rely on when they need a hand.

DEDICATED EMPLOYEES

Etsy has more than 600 dedicated staff members whose primary job is to make the Etsy marketplace and e-commerce experience rewarding for you and your customers. For example, the merchandising team continuously surveys the Etsy marketplace and shares findings with potential customers in a variety of ways, and Etsy's editors curate lists of suggested buys according to themes like "Valentine's Day collection," "spring collection," and "great guy gifts," to mention just a few. This team also puts a spotlight on particular lists of products according to categories like "mobile accessories" and "jewelry." The editors are also the folks behind *Etsy Finds*, a digital newsletter filled with buying suggestions for subscribers.

ETSY TASTEMAKERS

Beyond Etsy's employees, there are Etsy Tastemakers— groups and brands as diverse as the Brown University Alumni Association, *Lucky* magazine, and Whole Foods Market—who create a presence on Etsy with pages of curated suggestions. At present there are more than 225 Tastemakers in categories including "weddings," "lifestyle," "fashion," "family," "do-it-yourself (DIY)," and "art and design."

PURCHASING DATA

Information about what people are buying is a significant force in driving traffic to particular shops because this information, by definition, shows what people want and why they're willing to pay for it. Etsy's home page features direct links to the items that people want most and to the shops that carry those items. These coveted links on the home page create even more opportunities for sellers to connect with eager customers.

CURATED LISTS

You can't control whether Etsy's editors highlight your work, and there's no guarantee that your product will find a place in the curated lists generated by Tastemakers or purchasing data, but you can influence buyers' choices by becoming and remaining active in the Etsy community. You can start a discussion in a forum, comment on featured products and shops, and become a curator yourself.

Curated lists on Etsy receive thousands of page views. By adding your compliments, insights, and contributions to the comments section of a curated list, you increase the chances that someone will notice your shop. And when you take the time to curate your own list of favorites, you automatically create the opportunity for someone to click through to you and your product. Think of participation in the Etsy community as an investment in marketing. It's well worth the time you'll spend.

TEAMS

Sellers whose products are connected by a similar theme or who are living and working in the same region can find one another on Etsy and form a team. After all, when you're browsing online for an item, you seldom stop your search after viewing the products of a single seller. That's the logic behind Etsy teams: Every seller on the team has the same target audience, so when team members work together and promote each other's products, everyone on the team ultimately

ETSY – A TIMELINE

JUN
2005

ROBERT KALIN, THE COMPANY'S FIRST CEO;
CHRIS MAGUIRE; HAIM SCHOPPIK; AND JARED
TARBELL LAUNCH ETSY IN BROOKLYN, NEW YORK

DEC
2007

ETSY HAS NEARLY 450,000 REGISTERED SELLERS
GENERATING 26 MILLION IN ANNUAL SALES

SEP
2008

CHAD DICKERSON BECOMES ETSY'S FIRST CTO

JUL
2011

CHAD DICKERSON REPLACES KALIN AS ETSY'S CEO;
THE COMPANY REPORTS $500 MILLION IN REVENUE

OCT
2013

UNIQUE FACTORY-MANUFACTURED ITEMS ARE
ADMITTED UNDER ETSY'S NEW GUIDELINES

DEC
2014

ETSY'S REGISTERED USERS TOTAL 54 MILLION

JUN
2014

MIKE GRISHAVER JOINS ETSY AS DIRECTOR OF PRODUCT
TO LEAD THE COMPANY'S MOBILE INITIATIVES

MAR
2015

ETSY FILES FOR INITIAL PUBLIC OFFERING

APRIL
2015

ETSY GOES PUBLIC, RAISING OVER $278 MILLION AND
GIVING THE COMPANY A VALUE OF OVER $3.5 BILLION

garners more page views. Meanwhile, the prospective buyer enjoys a wider range of reliable choices. Everybody wins!

TECHNOLOGY

Etsy's technology has leveled the e-commerce playing field for sellers in remarkable ways. Etsy's platform can handle translations, currency exchanges, and transactions across an array of devices. Etsy can also take charge of bureaucratic matters like payment processing, shipping labels, coupons, and other things that arts-and-crafts types often find overwhelming.

SPECIAL PROGRAMS

Etsy Wholesale has built bridges between Etsy's sellers and the buyers who work for popular retail giants. Hello Etsy is a large face-to-face conference for sellers and small-business owners. Etsy also offers classes in entrepreneurial skills in various cities, and an entire area of the Etsy site is dedicated to bringing buyers face-to-face with Etsy sellers at flea markets and boutiques.

SETTING GOALS

You may have grown comfortable thinking of yourself as a crafter or a collector of vintage items, and that's fine—it's a big part of who you are. But with an Etsy shop up and running, you also need to start seeing yourself as a small-business owner, an entrepreneur with a brand to promote. This means thinking deeply and intelligently about the products you sell, how you present them, and how you communicate about what you're selling.

It's true that once in a while lightning strikes, and occasionally success comes through blind luck. Most of the time, though, people succeed on Etsy for concrete reasons. Successful Etsy shop owners have three things in common:

1. They know what they want to achieve.
2. They know how to break a large goal down into smaller, achievable actions.
3. They know how to create and maintain a vision of their goals.

DECIDE WHAT YOU WANT FROM YOUR ETSY SHOP

What do you want to achieve in your Etsy shop? Where do you see your brand in a year? How about in five years? If you can't come up with answers to these questions, then you haven't set the compass for your shop's success, which means establishing a recognizable brand, developing plenty of return customers and referrals, and generating the most essential element of a sustainable business—profits.

Consider the following aspects of your shop and your activities as an Etsy seller.

PURPOSE

Is there a purpose behind your shop? Do your products stand for something? This "something" could be a national or ethnic heritage, the environment, a way of being in the world, or any other theme or driving force that is meaningful to you.

PRODUCT LINE

Look at all the items you have for sale. Do they form a recognizable set? Do they have a common look and feel? Do they complement one another? If someone purchases more than one of your items, will that buyer be able to display them in the same room or wear them as elements of the same outfit?

PRODUCT FUNCTION

Do all your products serve a particular purpose for potential buyers? For example, if your buyer is a quilter or a collector of vintage baseball caps, can she go to your shop and expect to find the special item she wants?

PRODUCTION PROCESS

Is your production process as efficient as it could be? Are you ordering your materials in the most cost-effective way? Are

you paying attention to cost-effectiveness without com-
promising quality? Have you streamlined your packaging and
shipping processes? Also keep in mind that Etsy has direct
channels to manufacturers, making larger production lines a
possibility for you.

PRESENTATION

You have exactly one chance to make a first impression, so
make it a good one. Are you describing your product accurately? Are you giving buyers information about the materials
you use? Are photographs of your items professional, engaging, and consistent with your product line's look and feel?
Are you using the same logo, colors, and type style for your
shop, your packing slips, and your e-mails? Do your product
descriptions include selling points above and beyond those
conveyed by your product's name and the quality of your
photographs?

MARKETING

It's up to you to bring qualified traffic to your shop, which
means reaching out to every person who is not just willing but
actually ready and eager to buy your product. Later sections
of this book include information about fine-tuning your
customer-attraction strategies (for example, see Mastering
Keywords [page 54], Tagging for Success [page 58], and
Marketing on Social Media [page 77] in part 2). For now,
have you considered advertising with sites and services like
Facebook and Google AdWords? If you have a Facebook or

Twitter account, are you using those platforms to promote your product?

CUSTOMER SERVICE

Are you prompt, polite, generous, and personable when you interact with buyers or potential buyers? Your attitude toward customers has a direct and measurable effect on repeat business and referrals from others.

ENGAGEMENT WITH THE ETSY COMMUNITY

There's a lot to say about what Etsy can do for you (for example, see Making the Most of Etsy's Tools [page 66] and Making Connections [page 86] in part 2). Here's the short version: Every time you make yourself visible in any way on the Etsy site, there's a chance that someone will visit your shop and become a valued customer.

Have you started any conversations in an Etsy chat room? If so, are you willing to continue and to leave comments on other Etsy conversations?

Have you created or commented on a curated list, especially one likely to interest your potential buyers? Have you commented on a featured shop whose owners are in your field? Visitors to featured shops are also your potential buyers because when you comment on a featured shop, a link is created to your shop.

Have you joined a team of Etsy sellers with products similar or complementary to yours? Don't be scared off by a scarcity mentality. You and your colleagues will be working together to create a pool of potential buyers—and the truth is, there's more than enough business to go around.

OFFLINE PRESENCE

What about adding some face-to-face contact with potential customers? Etsy has tons of resources for promoting Etsy shops out in the world, so think about creating a presence for your product at flea markets and trade shows as well as in local boutiques. Major brick-and-mortar retailers are within your reach, too, because Etsy has strong relationships with buyers from stores like Nordstrom.

CREATE AND REACH MILESTONES

No goal ever achieved itself, and goals are seldom realized overnight. Most realistic goals consist of small, achievable, measurable action steps—milestones—and milestones in turn are made up of completed tasks, some so minor that you might be tempted to let them slide or skip them altogether. But don't!

The secret to achieving milestones, and then goals, lies in not becoming overwhelmed. And you can avoid becoming overwhelmed by setting priorities for the tasks you need to complete on the way to a particular milestone, and on the road to your ultimate goal.

- **WHICH TASKS DO YOU NEED TO COMPLETE ONLY ONCE IN ORDER TO REACH A PARTICULAR MILESTONE?** Examples might be hiring a designer to improve your logo, replacing one material with another to lower your production costs, or

STATE YOUR GOALS AS ACTION STEPS

Small steps in the right direction add up to big results!

CHOOSE AN AREA FOR EXPANSION. For example, you may decide to come up with a new product.

CREATE A PRECISE GOAL. For example, you may commit yourself to begin selling your new product by the end of next quarter.

CREATE A BREAKDOWN OF THE ACTIONS YOU'LL TAKE TO MEET THIS GOAL. For example, you may decide that the action steps are to brainstorm the most logical extensions of your product line, check out the competition, do research on the materials you'll need, make a prototype, introduce some efficiencies in production, create an inventory of the new product, photograph the product, tag it, describe it, and sell it.

reorganizing an area of your office to streamline your packing and shipping processes.

- **WHICH TASKS DO YOU NEED TO COMPLETE OVER AND OVER AGAIN?** Examples of recurring tasks might be participating in Etsy chats, commenting on curated lists, creating your own curated lists, ordering supplies, packing and shipping items, or building and improving your photographic skills.

The key to getting tasks completed, and getting them completed on time, is to put them on a schedule. You may have one schedule for recurring tasks—those that you perform daily, once weekly, twice weekly, or monthly—and another, more comprehensive schedule where you put your one-off tasks and set a date for their completion.

For daily tasks, maybe one hour in the morning is the perfect time, or the hour after lunch, or a 45-minute slot before you go to sleep. If running your Etsy shop already accounts for the largest part of your workday, then you can dedicate even more time to meeting your goals.

Here are two tips to keep in mind when you're creating milestones and priorities:

1. You can accomplish a great deal in a small amount of time, whether you're working on a recurring task or chipping away at a larger one. You don't have to wait until you have a free weekend or a whole week without other obligations.

2. Put every one of your tasks on your calendar, assign every task a specific time when it will have your full attention, and hold yourself accountable for honoring that commitment.

NURTURE A VISION

The first step in nurturing a vision is to dream big. Imagine things as they could be. The following worksheet will help you do just that. First look at the statements, and then write down whatever comes to mind. Take the lid off! This is your chance to envision the best of everything for yourself.

MY DREAM SHOP LOOKS AND FEELS LIKE . . .

MY PERFECT SHOP SELLS . . .

MY FUTURE CUSTOMERS ARE . . .

CUSTOMERS ASSOCIATE MY SHOP WITH ESTABLISHED BRANDS LIKE . . .

MY SHOP EARNS ME $ _____ IN SALES (PER MONTH, WEEK, DAY, HOUR)

I SPEND _____ HOURS (PER MONTH, WEEK, DAY) CREATING MY PRODUCTS

I SPEND _____ HOURS (PER MONTH, WEEK, DAY) MARKETING MY PRODUCTS

I ENGAGE WITH THE ETSY COMMUNITY BY . . .

I AM FEATURED ON THESE CURATED LISTS:

MY ETSY SHOP EARNS ME ENOUGH MONEY FOR ME TO HAVE _____ HOURS
OF FREE TIME (PER MONTH, WEEK, DAY) THAT I CAN USE TO DO THESE
THINGS IN THE REST OF MY LIFE:

YOUR VISION BOARD

A vision board can be a great tool for inspiration. Did you know that if you love the ocean, then looking at a picture of the ocean will prompt your brain to secrete the same "joy" hormones it would release if you were standing at the water's edge? In other words, whether you're looking at a picture of the ocean or standing ankle-deep in salt water, your brain and your hormones can't really tell the difference. The lesson here is that if you want your brain to believe in some desirable possibility, the first step is to put a pictorial representation of the desired outcome on display. Then look at it every day, and plant the seed of that possibility in your reality.

That's how you'll create your Etsy vision board: with as much visual accuracy and imagination as you can muster. Create, in the form of one or more images, a representation of what you want—your dream, your ideal—no holds barred. The vision board can contain words, magazine cutouts, printouts from your computer, and quotes from friends or famous people.

Consider using an image of yourself creating your Etsy items in an orderly, creative space; participating in Etsy forums; or attending outdoor trade shows. Include pictures of happy customers, a map of the locations where they live, the words *featured* and *most popular* displayed on your shop or next to your items, and dollar amounts for your monthly sales. And don't forget to add the Etsy logo and images of your Etsy shop.

Start putting into your consciousness a precise vision of how you'd like things to be—and keep your eye on the prize!

- ☐ **BIG VISION.** Create your ultimate goal.
- ☐ **MASTER LIST.** Write down everything you need to do.
- ☐ **LIST SEGMENTATION.** Divide your lists into areas of action.
- ☐ **ONE-OFF VERSUS ONGOING TASKS.** Distinguish single tasks from recurring actions.
- ☐ **LIST PRIORITIZATION.** Set priorities for what needs to happen when.
- ☐ **MASTER SCHEDULE.** Create a schedule for immediate one-time actions and ongoing, recurring tasks.

WHAT KIND OF
ETSY USER ARE YOU?

As a shop owner, it's important for you to use Etsy yourself so you can gain an experiential perspective on the buyer's perspective. Once you go to the site, search for items, and see what comes up, you'll also have a better sense of your competition and of how to phrase your own item tags, which directly affect Etsy search results. So get thee to the marketplace, and hunt around. Experiment with making purchases and really getting inside the buyer's head. What changes would you make if you were selling to yourself? What changes would you make if you were selling to a friend? Dive in, think only as a consumer, make some purchases, and do your due diligence as a researcher.

First, choose a type of item to buy:

- Search for this item.
- Experiment with different search terms, and notice what items come up.

Then visit different links and notice what compels you to buy:

- What do you respond to in the descriptions?
- What types of photographs make the biggest impact on you?
- Is there a price point that loses you?
- Do you feel willing to pay more?

Now contact a few shop owners, make a special request or two, and notice their responses:

- Did they reply right away?
- Were they accommodating?
- Did their tone seem distracted or defensive?

When it's time to make your purchase, buy two items of the same kind from two different sellers:

- Did one ship faster?
- Do you prefer one type of packaging over the other?
- Did either seller include an incentive for a future purchase?

Finally, evaluate your experience as a consumer:

- Would you purchase from this seller again?
- Do you feel compelled to search for other types of items on Etsy?
- Do you want to leave any comments at the seller's Etsy shop?

LEARNING FROM ETSY SELLERS' TOP 10 MISTAKES

Much of your Etsy shop's success will depend on the desirability of your product, your presence in the Etsy community, your visibility in search results, and your ability to make the sale when a prospective buyer finds your product. Here is your chance to learn from the 10 most frequent mistakes that successful Etsy sellers report prevented their shops from being noticed by curators, becoming customer favorites, being featured by Etsy's staff, and generating significant and consistent profits.

1. **BEING ABSENT FROM COMMUNITY FORUMS.** Maybe you see participation in Etsy's community forums and chats as manipulative, or maybe you believe you have nothing to contribute. Or it could be that you're not interested or simply think you don't have the time. But the fact remains that your participation is an essential requirement for driving traffic to your shop, raising your visibility, and increasing the chances that your shop will find its way onto a curated list or be featured in some other way.

2. **USING INACCURATE ITEM TAGS OR TAGLINES.** If a potential buyer finds your item through a search but decides not to buy it, the problem may be your item tags (the descriptive words or phrases attached to your product) or taglines (the short sentences or bits of text that convey the essence

of your brand and describe your target audience). Some item tags or taglines may be misleading. For example, have you tagged your knitted socks for infants as "footwear," which the buyer may associate with high-end designer shoes for men? Other tags may use terms that don't match the exact words the buyer is using (the buyer types "sunglasses," for example, but the only tag you've used for that item is "eyewear"). When a tag doesn't describe a product accurately, the product is effectively invisible to a potential buyer. Your tags need to reflect the search terms that buyers actually use.

3. **IGNORING OR MISUSING SEO.** Search engine optimization, or SEO, includes everything you do with keywords, tags, and taglines to make your products match up with as many customer searches as you can. SEO has a part to play in your product descriptions, posts on your social media pages, your blog posts, and the comments you leave on featured Etsy shops and in Etsy chat rooms. When you use SEO properly, search engines pick up your keywords, tags, and taglines and direct potential buyers to the items you have for sale.

4. **PHOTOGRAPHING ITEMS POORLY.** Mistakes in this category include blurred or low-resolution images, images that are too small, outdated images, distracting use of models, mismatched or outdated backgrounds, and misrepresentation of an item's true color. There's nothing like a low-quality, unprofessional photograph to kill a potential sale.

5. **WRITING UNPROFESSIONAL PRODUCT DESCRIPTIONS.** It's possible to get a buyer all the way to the checkout page and then lose the sale. Why does this happen? Maybe the product description isn't specific enough—or maybe it's way too specific when all the customer wants is the product, not a long-winded account of its origins and manufacturing process. Another issue is that there may be a mismatch between the unprofessional sound of a product description and the professional look of the item's photograph. A discrepancy like that leaves the would-be buyer suspecting that the product is less sophisticated or of lower quality than its photograph makes it appear. And it's not always a good idea to let buyers know exactly how homegrown a product is. Buyers know perfectly well that Etsy shops are run by independent entrepreneurs, but they don't necessarily need to know that your workshop is the cobweb-filled bomb shelter your grandparents built in 1956. A customer about to part with hard-earned cash wants to feel confident about buying a high-quality item, a purchase on a par with the best of what's available from Amazon and other online sellers.

6. **OVERPRICING OR UNDERPRICING ITEMS.** If your prices are too high, you will lose sales. Your prices don't have to match those of your competitors, but if yours are significantly higher, you need to present a convincing reason for the difference, such as higher quality, superior craftsmanship, unique features, or an item's place in your collection as a whole. You can also set your prices so low that every

sale is guaranteed, but you may end up barely breaking even while working twice as hard as your competitors. Always check your motivation for cutting a price. Every time you lower your prices, you give your competitors a reason to lower theirs, and pretty soon it's a race to the bottom, with potential buyers also losing out as products become unavailable or shops go out of business.

7. **PRACTICING INEFFICIENT PRODUCTION.** Every aspect of your production operation must be streamlined if you want your shop to stay in business. Inefficiency in production may involve the time it takes to make an item as well as the time you spend buying supplies, packaging your wares, and dealing with shipping and handling. Production inefficiencies drive home the point that time is money, as they can become very expensive over time.

8. **OFFERING POOR CUSTOMER SERVICE.** Customer service involves everything about how you communicate with past buyers as well as those who still represent potential sales. Pay attention to your words and your tone in online chats, in e-mails, on your packing slip, and in your process for handling complaints, returns, and refunds. The quality of your packaging matters, too, and it has a huge impact on a customer's experience of your brand. The same goes for your shipping times, which depend not just on your shipping methods but also on how much inventory you have on hand. Remember, every customer is also a potential evangelist for your brand. You can't afford to lose or dissatisfy a single buyer who has trusted you with a purchase.

DON'T FORGET
THE GUYS

Are you losing sales because you're ignoring half your potential buyers? Maybe it's time to take a look at your product line and see if you can add some male-friendly items.

MATERIALS. Would a guy wear or buy an item made from this fabric?

COLORS. Is your product available in a shade that's appropriate for a man?

FONTS. Your product descriptions may be perfect, but is their frilly typographic presentation telling male shoppers to stay away?

9. **LACKING BRAND COHESION.** If your products are too diverse in their function or sensibility, your shop lacks brand cohesion. When your shop presents a unified look and feel, customers think of your brand first when they're in the market for an item you have for sale. An attractively cohesive brand can also inspire some impulse buying, prompting customers to check out with more items than they were consciously looking for or intended to buy.

10. **SELLING ITEMS OF POOR QUALITY OR WORKMANSHIP.** Even a single dissatisfied customer or negative review can have a long-lasting negative impact on your shop and your brand. So double-check your materials, and road test your products in real-life wear-and-tear situations. Toss your customized iPhone case in your purse, or set it on your car's dash. Wear your hand-crocheted belt with jeans and with a skirt. Fill your handwoven purse with bulky items, and throw it over your shoulder. Hang your fine art in the sun for a week, and see how the frame protects your work. User-test and get user feedback before you commit to the final version of your product. Never let your brand become associated with anything less than the highest level of quality and workmanship.

SELLER'S CORNER

ELLEN GIGGENBACH

ETSY SHOP: ELLEN GIGGENBACH
ETSY.COM/SHOP/ELLENGIGGENBACH

Ellen Giggenbach is a New Zealand–based artist and passionate paper crafter. In 2011 she launched her Etsy shop, Ellen Giggenbach, where she currently sells prints, DIY paper and fabric crafts, scarves, and wall decals, all showcasing her original artwork.

WHAT DO YOU WISH YOU HAD KNOWN WHEN YOU STARTED YOUR ETSY SHOP?

At the beginning, I was selling just a few original pieces of art, which didn't work for me. Offering the same work as an affordable print transformed my shop. I underestimated just how important it was to offer my customers affordable price points. Now that I do, I often sell more than one item with each sale.

HAVE YOU MADE ANY CHANGES TO YOUR ETSY SHOP THAT YIELDED TANGIBLE POSITIVE RESULTS?

It took me a while to decide to make printables available because I worried there would be a risk that my other craft sales could suffer. This has actually proven to be the opposite. Giving buyers different options has definitely yielded positive results.

WHAT ACTIONS HAVE YOU TAKEN TO BOOST SALES?

The biggest thing I do to boost sales is regularly add new products and at the same time feature them on all my social media outlets. This in turn creates interest, and the item is often shared further, allowing new potential customers to discover my shop. I also regularly change my header depending on the season, which is also a good way to highlight a particular product. For instance, around Easter, I have my Easter paper craft featured on my shop banner.

WHAT ETSY TOOL DO YOU FIND PARTICULARLY HELPFUL?

I regularly check my stats, particularly if I've had a spike in sales. It's a great way to find out if one of my products has been featured somewhere. Having a listing featured on someone else's social media site has proven to be one of the best ways to increase awareness of my profile.

WHAT PIECE OF ADVICE WOULD YOU OFFER NEW ETSY SELLERS?

My very best advice is to spend almost as much time presenting your product as you did creating it! The love, care, and energy you take photographing and styling directly reflects the passion you have for creating your products. I often browse other shops and notice that some simply look more alive and full of passion than others.

PART

2

MAXIMIZE YOUR SALES ON ETSY

To create a financially successful Etsy shop, first think of your shop as a company. You'll want to maximize your company's sales. It doesn't just mean boosting your bottom line. It means making it into the most successful enterprise of its kind that it can possibly be.

With that goal in mind, this part homes in on how you present your shop and your products, whether cultivating an engaging voice or following best practices for photography.

It also shows you how to use keywords, tagging, and Etsy's proprietary tools so customers can find you, and then teaches you how to price and market your products in ways that enhance and complement your branding efforts.

Finally, you'll learn about making connections with other Etsy sellers, fine-tuning every aspect of your customer service, and expanding your shop's range of items.

CRAFTING A VOICE FOR YOUR SHOP

Every Etsy shop has a unique voice. The tone of your shop's voice is conveyed by your banner, your profile, and your product descriptions.

Your shop's voice can be whimsical, serious, or sophisticated. It can speak with a trendy, homegrown, or old-fashioned "accent." But remember that whatever tone you choose for your shop's voice—and you should make sure this choice is a conscious one—it will automatically communicate some kind of mood or feeling to your shop's visitors.

And that's very important. Everything about your shop's voice contributes to potential buyers' perceptions of what your brand stands for. Make sure your banner, profile, and product descriptions work in concert to present a unified voice.

BURNISH YOUR BANNER

Your banner is your shop's entryway. It represents your brand and sets the tone for your whole shop. The colors and fonts you choose, the images you display, and your use of white space all contribute to a visitor's experience of your shop and influence the visitor's desire to browse, buy, come back, and refer other buyers. You want your banner to be welcoming, informative, and relevant to your brand.

ESSENTIALS AND OPTIONS

There's actually only one essential for your banner, but it's a big one, and it's nonnegotiable: the name of your shop. After all, your shop's name is your brand! Once you've met that requirement, you can consider the following options—but don't overdo it, or you'll risk overwhelming your brand.

- Your name, unless already part of your shop's name (as in "Designs by Jane Doe")
- A tagline, to tell visitors in the simplest terms what your brand is all about
- A photograph of yourself to personalize your shop
- Your shop's logo
- A link to your website
- Images (for example, photographs of your items, backgrounds used in your photographs, drawings, fine art, graphics, cartoons)
- Behind-the-scenes images of your workspace, including materials and items at various stages of production
- A quote that sums up your mission (for example, something about the items you have for sale or about how you hope customers will benefit from a purchase)
- Blocks of color to subdivide your banner

TEST RUNS AND EXPERIMENTS

To some extent, a banner is always a matter of personal taste. But every one of your banner's components expresses your brand, so it's a good idea to run your ideas past people whose opinions you respect, and it's smart to find out how your banner will look to people viewing it within various digital environments.

- Try different banners out on friends, colleagues, and even strangers. Create three choices, and ask for honest feedback. What impressions of your shop do people form when they look at different versions of your banner? What moods or feelings do they report?
- Experiment with different banners on your Etsy site, and see whether your traffic and sales change with each one. Switch things up! Rotate three banners over three weeks, and compare your results.
- View your banner on various platforms (a mobile phone, a tablet, a laptop screen, a desktop monitor) to make sure it holds up without distortion in spite of variations in screen size and display mode.

POLISH YOUR PROFILE

Think of your profile as a personal conversation between you and your current or potential customers. It gives you an opportunity to invite them in and draw them closer. Tell them about yourself—where you live, how you spend your days, and what inspired you to open your shop.

Visitors want to feel as if they know you, so anticipate their questions:

- What motivates you?
- What sets you apart?
- How long have you been crafting these items or selling these products?
- What plans do you have for your shop over the next few months?

Your profile is not the place to express insecurity about your product or your artistic abilities. Make your profile a self-doubt-free zone!

WRITE WINNING PRODUCT DESCRIPTIONS

People buy things for all kinds of reasons. They have practical needs for particular items, they're looking for an experience of some kind, or they want to be cool, get noticed, or feel taken care of. Turn your product descriptions into promises to meet potential customers' practical or emotional needs.

Be honest. Don't promise that a jar of shea butter will erase forty years from a septuagenarian's skin or bring a teenager true and lasting love. But don't be afraid to talk about the care you've put into creating that product or to suggest that the same loving care will be transferred to the customer in the form of a luscious, sensuous, delightfully fragrant product that makes her feel special and pampered. And you'll certainly want to let visitors to your shop know if an item is a one-of-a-kind treasure or was produced as part of a limited edition.

Customers like to feel they're in the know and on the cutting edge. When you make an item seem special, the people who buy it feel special, too.

Use product descriptions to promote your brand. Is a particular item also sold in stores? Has anyone written an article about the item for a blog or featured it on one of Etsy's curated lists? You want to make the sale, of course, but a product description is not just for getting the customer to your checkout page as quickly as possible. A description can also refer buyers to your profile as well as to relevant articles or blog posts about your products. This type of rich descriptive material has the potential to keep a shopper on your site, engage her with your content, and encourage her to browse (and maybe buy) more items than the one that originally attracted her to your shop.

Remind the buyer to let you know if a purchase will be a gift, since that will affect whether you include an invoice with the shipment. Maybe you offer a gift-wrapping option, too. Or maybe your basic presentation is already so gorgeous that the item needs no special presentation at all. Let the buyer know! Promising a great presentation can make the difference between making the sale and losing it to a competitor. Also be sure to let customers know if you offer custom designs or are able to accommodate special requests.

You may want to include information about how a product was assembled, where the materials came from, how the elements were chosen, and how the product has evolved to meet customers' needs. Some sellers refer buyers to a list of frequently asked questions (FAQs) as a way of establishing expectations and preventing disappointment and returns. Others use their product descriptions for clarifications and disclosures to make sure these are read. Clarifications and disclosures often have to do with the following areas:

- SHIPPING. Give a full explanation of your shipping options, including various prices, when products ship (within 24 hours, within 5 days, in 2 weeks), how long delivery takes (one day, five days, one month), which carriers you use (FedEx, UPS, US Postal Service), and whether the shipment will be local, interstate, or international.
- RETURN POLICY. Give a full and specific explanation of your policy. Remember, though, that it's better to lose a sale than have to accept a return, so make every effort to ensure that your product descriptions are complete, accurate, and unlikely to raise unrealistic expectations.
- CUSTOMERS' LIKELY ASSUMPTIONS. Be sure to say what is and is not included with the product. If it's a photograph, does it come with a frame? Do the sunglasses come with a case? Does a shirt come with spare buttons? Does a robot toy come with batteries?
- WEAR AND TEAR. Be forthcoming about whether exposure to sunlight or moisture, use during vigorous exercise, rough handling, or other factors are likely to impede the performance of an item or shorten a product's expected life cycle.

- **FABRICS.** Offer a full explanation of the fabrics used in an item, the variations that may occur, instructions for laundering or dry cleaning, and any necessary cautions about allergic reactions.
- **SIZES.** Refer the customer to a size chart, explain how to use it, mention any relevant variations, and say whether washing or drying will affect a garment's fit.
- **COLORS.** Explain that the photograph of an item in your shop, as viewed on the customer's screen, may not reproduce the item's exact color.

ACTION STEPS

☐ **BANNER.** Create an attractive banner that represents the look and feel of your brand.

☐ **PROFILE.** Create an inviting and truthful profile that is both welcoming and confident.

☐ **PRODUCT DESCRIPTIONS.** Write about your product in an honest but enticing way that seals the deal with every potential customer.

10 TIPS FOR WRITING EFFECTIVE PRODUCT DESCRIPTIONS

1. **CONVINCE.** Intensify buyers' interest in your product. Describe it in a way that makes buyers feel they can't live without it.

2. **AMAZE.** Is your item one of a kind? Is it rare? Vintage? Describe why this product is so amazing.

3. **WOW.** Use the product description to mention any press coverage of your item. Has a celebrity bought your item? Has someone featured it in a curated list? Is the item linked to in any articles? Showcase how special your items are.

4. **ENTICE.** Let viewers know they can create a custom order or modify what they see. Reel them in with your artistry, and let it work on them.

5. **EDUCATE.** Explain how the product was made, the choices you made along the way, and the materials you used.

6. **PREPARE.** Let your buyer know how wear and tear, along with weather, washing, and normal use, will affect the product. Alert buyers to any color discrepancies or potential variations. Prevent avoidable disappointment!

7. ANTICIPATE. Explain exactly what is included with the product, and address typical questions about this sort of item. If it's a watch, for example, does it come with batteries? Does the typewriter come with a case? Don't force buyers to take their time, and yours, just to ask for basic information that you can easily provide in your product description.

8. EXPLAIN. Detail all shipping options as well as options for returning a product. Include specifications for shipping domestically as well as internationally.

9. ANSWER. Link to your frequently asked questions (FAQs) so buyers' concerns and questions will be thoroughly addressed.

10. DELIVER. Explain how the product will arrive, and include information about options for gift delivery, including gift wrapping and separate packaging of the invoice.

IMPROVING YOUR PHOTOGRAPHS

High-quality photographs indicate a high-quality product. Studying your product's photograph is the closest an online buyer can get to picking the product up and examining it in person.

Don't let your product be sold short by a photograph that falls short. Take advantage of these insider tips for shooting professional-grade product photos.

1. **COVER EVERY ANGLE.** You want to give your shop's visitors a fluid experience. Prospective buyers should be able to imagine holding, turning, and inspecting an item as they click through your photos.

2. **SHOOT HIGH RESOLUTION IMAGES.** If the item in your photograph becomes grainy or pixelated when a visitor enlarges it onscreen, you'll probably lose the sale. You want the highest resolution possible so prospective buyers can make the image as large as they want it.

3. **CHOOSE THE OPTIMUM BACKGROUND.** The background you choose gives the buyer more information about your brand. Your background says, "This product belongs in this environment. If you purchase this product, you are entitled to this environment as well." Consider featuring your product alongside an ornate block of marble or a vase of flowers, or against a forest or desert scene.

4. **USE BRIGHT LIGHTING.** Lighting can make your product shine or leave it looking flat and dull. Avoid glare. Consider using natural lighting, whether outdoors or in a sunny room. A white porcelain bathtub provides a soft white background. You can also use a professional light box.

5. **SHOOT TRUE TO COLOR.** The color of the item in the photograph must resemble the item's actual color as closely as possible. Alert buyers if large discrepancies are unavoidable.

6. **SHOOT TRUE TO SIZE.** Photograph your item next to some common, highly recognizable item so the buyer gets a realistic idea of the item's size.

7. **USE A MODEL.** Models sell products. If appropriate, use a model in your photo, and go as professional as you can. Study magazines and catalogs that sell products comparable to yours, and note what you like and don't like about their use of models.

8. **PAY ATTENTION TO UNIFORMITY AND CONSISTENCY.** You should regard each one of your product photographs as one element of a collection. Your photographs, when laid out as a set, should make up a uniform portfolio. Together they should promote one brand, one look, one feel, and one consistent product line.

9. **FEATURE UNIQUE PRESENTATIONS.** For extra flair, dress your set. Consider photographing your item next to a distinct prop—a bowling ball, for example, or a phone booth,

a typewriter, or a hurricane lamp. Think of this as an opportunity to take a step or two outside the box without alienating potential customers.

10. **REMEMBER LIFESTYLE RELEVANCE.** When you place your item in a real-life setting, your customer can easily associate your product with his daily life. A lifestyle-relevant photograph makes your item seem more accessible.

Take a risk. Be unique. You're swimming in a sea of amazing Etsy sellers. Stand out, and capture the prize.

ACTION STEPS

☐ **SET THE STAGE.** Select the best lighting, models, and backgrounds you can afford. Let your products shine.

☐ **CLICK WITH PURPOSE.** Shoot your products from every angle, and give the buyer a realistic experience of what it will feel like to touch and hold an item.

☐ **BE CLEVER.** Create a unique background environment to set your product apart. From models to props, invest in high-quality supportive items to showcase your product. Your photographs need to entice your buyer and make the sale.

MASTERING KEYWORDS

The role of keywords is absolutely fundamental—they make your products visible to potential buyers.

Search engines all across the Internet find keywords tucked into product descriptions and present exact matches to people who are searching for those products. You definitely want your items popping up in potential customers' search results!

KNOW YOUR KEYWORDS

There are two kinds of keywords:

1. Short-tail (generic) keywords are made up of single terms ("wallets") or brief multiple-word terms ("leather wallets").

2. Long-tail keywords use multiple terms, longer phrases, or specific strings of words ("religious figure leather wallets").

Short-tail keywords will get you more traffic, but long-tail keywords will get you more sales because these keywords bring you qualified traffic, or visits from buyers who are committed to finding exactly what you sell and are usually ready to make a purchase.

Let's say you're selling leather wallets embossed with images of religious figures, but the only keyword you're using is the short-tail keyword "leather wallets." Someone who types "leather wallets" into Google's search engine will be presented with a link to your Etsy site—and about 16.5 million additional Web pages.

But if you were to use the long-tail keyword "religious figure leather wallets," Google would return a link to your Etsy shop and only 2.8 million other Web pages—still a long shot, but with much better odds of a sale. And the more specific you can get, the more your prospects improve ("religious figure leather wallets Saint Anselm" returns a link to your shop and only about 26,000 other sellers of this particular item).

Besides being very, very specific in your use of long-tail keywords, the trick is to find out exactly what keywords people are typing into search engines when they go on the hunt for particular items, and then get feedback on how effective your keywords are. See the Resources at the end of this book for links to Google AdWords, Google Analytics, and HubSpot Keyword Grader, sophisticated tools that will analyze the flow of traffic to your Etsy site and let you know which of your current keywords are driving that traffic.

USE YOUR KEYWORDS

You can use keywords in many places, and you should put them wherever you can:

- In the name of your Etsy shop
- On your shop's banner
- In your shop's tagline
- In the names, descriptions, and taglines of the items you have for sale
- In the labels of your product photographs

- In your Etsy profile
- On your social media pages (Facebook, Twitter, Tumblr, Instagram, Pinterest)
- In articles and blog posts that you write for other websites

You can stuff quite a few phrases into a single product name, so don't be shy about calling a product something like "Long White Bridal Veil; Traditional Cathedral Veil; Long Wedding Veil; Lace Trim Veil." By giving your item this name, you increase your chances of attracting a number of customers who are looking for the same product but using different keywords to search for it.

In your product description, however, you won't call this item "Long White Bridal Veil; Traditional Cathedral Veil; Long Wedding Veil; Lace Trim Veil." Instead, you'll craft a description along these lines: "This long white bridal veil is made with a traditional cathedral wedding in mind. Its lace trim will beautifully complement the bride's wedding gown."

See how that works? This natural-sounding product description uses keywords that effectively attract customers who are looking for what you have to offer.

ACTION STEPS

☐ KNOW. Identify the keywords used by potential customers who are looking for items similar to your product.

☐ LIST. Make a list of long-tail keywords, and rank these terms in order of their effectiveness.

☐ USE. Insert your most effective keywords everywhere you can.

YOUR ETSY PODCAST PLAYLIST

The Etsy podcasts, a free collection of interviews with Etsy sellers, showcase the diversity and excellence embodied in the Etsy community. Listen while you're working or wait until you're relaxing at night. Here are the nine podcasts you can't live without, all available here: http://itunes.apple.com/us/podcast/etsy/id274681115.

ETSY TEAMS EMPOWERING COMMUNITIES: ROCKFORD AND BEYOND. A collection of ideas about how to make an Etsy team work for you.

HOW-TUESDAY: UPCYCLED GIFT WRAP. Get creative with gift wrapping.

HOW-TUESDAY: GET THINGS DONE. Maximize your time and productivity as your own boss.

HANDMADE PORTRAITS: THE PAPERCUTTING OF ROB RYAN. Find beauty in simple things.

HANDMADE PORTRAITS: FASHION DESIGNER RIORDAN ROACHE. Discover elegant textures in a designer's sophisticated line.

THE TIES THAT BIND: AYSEGUL & SEBAHAT. Meet a mother-and-daughter team from Turkey.

A LETTERPRESS LEGACY WITH LUCKY DUCK PRESS. Meet Patrick Barrett, who uses a foot-powered printing press in the tradition of his great-grandfather, founder of Sterling Press in 1901.

THERE'S NO PLACE LIKE HERE: PASS THE BATON. Discover vintage Japanese items from a Tokyo consignment shop.

LEANNE MARSHALL TAKES ON FASHION WEEK. New York fashion at its best.

TAGGING FOR SUCCESS

A tag, as mentioned earlier, is a word or a phrase that describes your product in the simplest terms. When you list an item on Etsy, you can identify it with up to 13 tags. Be sure to use all 13. Every time you use fewer than 13 tags, you decrease the chances that your item will pop up in a customer's product search. By the same token, every tag you use gives you one more chance for your product to be discovered. Your tags also determine how easily your items can be found with Etsy's search bar and in Etsy's browsing pages and categories.

How do you find the best tags for your items? In addition to researching keywords with utilities like Google AdWords, Google Analytics, and HubSpot Keyword Grader, you can use the Etsy search bar to discover the words and phrases that actual customers are entering to find the products they want. Just type your idea for a tag into the Etsy search bar, and the search bar will begin to display the words and phrases that Etsy's customers are using for their searches. These are the words and phrases you should use for your item tags.

To reach as many different kinds of buyers as possible, you also need to add some variety to your tags. For example, if you are selling a brown leather belt with a vintage brass buckle that has a horse design etched into it, you could tag your item "brown leather belt" to attract buyers who are interested in a brown leather belt but are indifferent to the kind of buckle that comes with it. But if you tag it "vintage brass buckle belt," you'll invite buyers who are specifically seeking a vintage buckle but may be less concerned with the accompanying belt. And to attract this item's most qualified traffic, the tag "vintage horse buckle belt" will speak to all the equestrians who have their hearts set on this type of belt and this type of buckle.

Here is an example of how to use 13 tags for an item:

1. Bridal veil

2. Wedding veil

3. Wedding bridal veil

4. Bridal wedding veil

5. Long wedding veil

6. Long bridal veil

7. Lace edge wedding veil

8. Lace edge bridal veil

9. Lace edge long wedding veil

10. Lace edge long bridal veil

11. Bridal veil with comb

12. Wedding veil with comb

13. Wedding veil white

Note that these tags don't include the words *accessory, wedding day,* or *bridal wear.* Such tags are too broad to target the audience you want to reach. As with long-tail keywords, it's better to be more specific and reach buyers who are serious about purchasing the item.

Here is another example of how to use the 13 tags Etsy allows for each item. In this case, you're creating tags for a gold-toned cuff-style metal bracelet stamped with an image of Our Lady of Guadalupe:

1. Our Lady of Guadalupe cuff bracelet
2. Religious jewelry
3. Mexican saints jewelry
4. Metal cuff bracelet
5. Cuff bracelet art
6. Cuff bracelet
7. Catholic saint jewelry
8. Catholic saint bracelet
9. Virgin of Guadalupe jewelry
10. Mexican Virgin Mary bracelet
11. Our Lady Guadalupe jewelry
12. Mexican saint bracelet
13. Cuff bracelet with design

Note that some of the tags include the religious reference and some do not. This is an example of diversification, which will attract buyers who are specifically looking for representations of Our Lady of Guadalupe in a piece of jewelry as well as customers who are looking for a cuff bracelet and may be pleasantly surprised to find one adorned with a religious figure.

Tagging doesn't stop with your products. You can also tag blog posts and articles you've written. Just as you did when you were trying out tags for your items, type a possible tag for a blog post or article into the Etsy search bar, and the bar will begin to display tags already in use by other Etsy sellers.

The importance of using precise, diverse tags cannot be overemphasized. Again, Etsy lets you use up to 13 for every item, blog post, or article, so don't pass up the chance to drive traffic to your shop.

ACTION STEPS

☐ GRAB THE MOST POPULAR TAGS FOR YOUR ITEM. Type the most relevant phrase into the Etsy search bar, and note the tags that automatically pop up.

☐ DIVERSIFY YOUR TAGS. Think broad and varied. Use tags to attract as many types of shoppers to your products as possible.

☐ USE 13 TAGS. For every tag you add, you increase the odds that your product will be pulled up in search results.

☐ TAG EVERYWHERE. Place tags for every item you carry as well as for every blog post and article you write.

SELLER'S CORNER

LENEY BREEDEN

ETSY SHOP: A GIRL NAMED LENEY
ETSY.COM/SHOP/AGIRLNAMEDLENEY

Leney Breeden is a knitwear designer and traveling photographer based in Virginia. In 2011 she launched her Etsy shop, A Girl Named Leney, where she sells knitwear of all kinds.

WHAT DO YOU WISH YOU HAD KNOWN WHEN YOU STARTED A GIRL NAMED LENEY?

That consistency is really important when it comes to your products, your photos of those products, and your communication with your customers. I also wish I'd known that it takes a good amount of time to curate and build a shop that you're proud of. It doesn't happen over night. It wasn't really until this past year that I felt truly content and proud of the work I was producing, consistency-wise and in terms of portraying the look and brand I wanted. It takes a lot of hard work and time. It's really easy to get caught up in comparing your shop to everyone else's, and it's something I struggle with from time to time. Something I heard once that's been the most beneficial for me in regard to being content with where I'm at is "You can't compare your beginning to someone else's middle." That was so huge for me, and it's so true. Everyone's journey is different.

HOW HAS ETSY HELPED YOU GROW YOUR BUSINESS?

Being a seller on Etsy has so many awesome benefits. There's a built-in community of people that you can collaborate with, turn to for advice, and chat with about challenges and successes. It's so great having a group of people to go to from all over the world who get what you're doing and are more than happy to give you advice. Etsy has also driven so much traffic to my shop. I don't know if I'd be able to say that I've sold my knits to twenty countries outside of the United States if it weren't for Etsy!

WHAT CHALLENGES HAVE YOU EXPERIENCED AS AN ETSY SHOP OWNER?

Underselling my work was a big challenge when I first started out. I didn't fully understand the value of handmade wares: how to properly price things according to your supply costs, how to be compensated appropriately for your labor and time. This especially came into play when I started getting wholesale offers. I quickly realized that I would hardly earn a profit at wholesale with my prices, which was a sign right there that I wasn't pricing properly.

WHAT CHANGES HAVE YOU MADE TO YOUR ETSY SHOP THAT YIELDED TANGIBLE POSITIVE RESULTS?

I think the biggest positive change was in my photos. I used to take all of my product photos myself; however, it limited me quite a bit. So I struck up a partnership with my extremely talented friend Meagan, who now takes all of my photos for me. I'm actually a photographer as well, but because I wanted to be able to style and model the pieces myself, photographing them too was just creating twice as much work. So now she photographs everything for me, and I don't have to worry about it, because I trust her 100 percent and know that we're on the same page. Ever since she's taken over photography, I've had nothing but increases in sales and revenue. So I would definitely say if you invest in anything, invest in a photographer! It is so worth it and will pay off in the long run. That and buying a shipping label printer and using an at-home shipping program. I cannot tell you how huge this was for me. I have saved *so* much time and money as a result, especially because I do ship internationally. I no longer have to stand in line at the post office to fill out customs forms and it's the greatest thing. I only wish I had started this system sooner!

WHAT ACTIONS HAVE YOU TAKEN TO BOOST SALES?

I've reached out to a few popular bloggers and had them promote my designs. I've also offered giveaways and coupons every so often. Mostly, I just try to be consistent in promoting my work, show people my creative process and what it looks like to be a knitwear designer behind the scenes. My Instagram (@agirlnamedleney) has been great for that, and I think it's really benefited my sales. People love seeing how my process works, which motivates and inspires me to create more.

DO YOU HAVE ANY TIPS FOR RETAINING RETURN CUSTOMERS?

Being really helpful and readily available for answering questions or concerns has definitely gotten me return customers. Some questions may seem silly, or even annoying if it's something you have already answered—whether in your listing, shop info, or policies—but people miss that stuff sometimes. If you're patient, helpful, and friendly in your responses, you'll build good, personable relationships with people who will enjoy working with you and want to be return buyers.

MAKING THE MOST
OF ETSY'S TOOLS

Shoppers come to a mall for shoes or shirts, and as they stroll past stores selling stationery and jewelry, they decide to make additional purchases. Meanwhile, the mall's owners provide shoppers with a parking lot, a map to all the stores, restrooms, and a food court—all amenities that keep people spending money at the mall.

Having a shop on Etsy is like owning a store in a mall. Etsy creates an attractive environment for prospective buyers by providing them with conveniences like shopping tips, lists of featured products and shops, and blogs.

Etsy also provides a number of very helpful resources for sellers. Take advantage of all these tools and resources that Etsy has created for you:

- **SHOP STATISTICS.** Etsy's Shop Stats, as they're called, are available to every Etsy seller. The Shop Stats offer data about the keywords buyers have used to arrive at your products. They also tell you where your page views are coming from, and they let you know which of your items have garnered the most views. If you see that more people are looking at your belts than at your wallets, this important information should influence your product development as well as the items you feature in your shop. The Shop Stats also tell you which of your tags are working. In addition, they show you how many times someone clicked through to your shop from a search result but failed to make a purchase. That's important information, too—maybe your keywords didn't really line up with the product, or the product description or photo turned the buyer off, or the price was too high or too low.

- **ETSY SEARCH BAR.** This search bar helps prospective customers find what they're looking for. It also enables sellers to perform market research (see Tagging for Success, page 58).
- **ETSY SELLER HANDBOOK.** This so-called handbook is actually a dynamic collection of blog posts containing advice from Etsy administrators, guest business experts, and Etsy sellers. It includes pointers on making your shop successful as well as updates on Etsy policies and other site-related news. Offering hot tips as well as nuts-and-bolts information about marketing, search visibility, and product photos, the handbook is available in multiple languages to accommodate the global nature of the Etsy marketplace and the sellers and buyers who use the Etsy site.
- **ETSY APP.** This application puts you, the seller, in regular communication with your customers, both directly (for example, when you use the app to answer a customer's question) and indirectly (as when you edit your item photos or receive notification that you've made a sale and that it's time to ship the item). The app is available for a number of platforms, including mobile phones and tablets.
- **SHIPPING LABELS.** Sellers in the United States who use PayPal or Etsy's Direct Checkout payment method can save

a trip to the post office by using this tool to buy and print US Postal Service shipping labels directly from their Etsy shops. The tool automatically provides a shipping record, a tracking number, and access to discounted postage rates.

- **LISTING VARIATIONS.** This tool lets you offer your customers a variety of options for a single product (color, size, fabric, flavor, scent, and so on). It also allows you to indicate that variations, such as ordering the item in a larger size or in leather instead of vinyl, increase the item's price.

- **COUPON CODES.** Etsy lets sellers use codes for three different types of coupons that they can make available to buyers: a code for a discount amounting to a flat percentage of an item's price, a code for a discount of a fixed dollar amount, and a code for free shipping.

- **TEAMS.** An Etsy team is a group of your fellow Etsy sellers with whom you can talk, share, strategize, and work to promote the shops of everyone on the team (see Understanding Possibilities and Avoiding Pitfalls, page 10).

- **FORUMS.** Etsy's forums offer a terrific opportunity for you to get educated about all things Etsy and build your presence on the site by participating in conversations. Forum discussions cover marketing tips, troubleshooting, social media, increasing sales, and many more topics of interest to sellers.

- **ETSY SUCCESS NEWSLETTER.** This twice-weekly electronic newsletter highlights sellers' tips from the *Seller Handbook* and includes topics such as branding, standing out from the competition, and growing your business.

☐ **EXPLORE.** Use Etsy's shop statistics to analyze your shop's performance.

☐ **EXPERIMENT.** Play around with Etsy's search bar, and see how relevant your items are. Adjust your tags and keywords accordingly.

☐ **DOWNLOAD.** Get your hands on the Etsy app, and increase your customer connectivity.

☐ **READ.** Get yourself a practical business education by checking out the Etsy *Seller Handbook* and archived Etsy Success newsletters.

☐ **USE.** Identify the right tools, such as Etsy's shipping labels, listing variations, and coupon codes.

☐ **ENGAGE.** Raise your profile in the Etsy community by joining teams and forums. The more you participate in the community, the more likely you are to be referred to and included in events for sellers.

PITCHING IDEAS TO ETSY'S
SELLER HANDBOOK

The *Seller Handbook* offers insider information that helps the Etsy community by describing best practices. As an Etsy shop owner, you have much to contribute, even if you feel like a total novice.

So how do you turn your experience, regrets as well as successes, into valuable content for someone else? Almost all sellers are struggling with some aspect of their shops, and most have questions and are open to advice. Consider starting your post with a problem other sellers can relate to. Write about what did not work to solve this problem, and then describe the solution you discovered. By sharing your challenges and your strategies for getting past roadblocks, you help other sellers solve their own problems. And when you write about your successes, you inspire your colleagues to reach their full potential.

Here are a few hot topics for you to pitch to Etsy's *Seller Handbook*:

YOUR BIGGEST REGRETS. What do you wish you'd done differently? Is something obvious to you now, even though it never occurred to you when you were starting out? For example, did you stifle your intuition about some product or issue, only to find out that you would have done better to follow it instead?

YOUR STRONGEST SELLERS. Why do sales for one of your items surpass sales for your other products? For your strongest seller, are you doing anything different in terms of production, packaging, promotion, or presentation?

YOUR CUSTOMER SERVICE SNAFUS. Have you survived a close encounter with a difficult customer? How did you deal with the justified wrath of a customer who felt wronged by a mistake you made? What did you do to repair the relationship?

YOUR BEST AND WORST REVIEWS. What did you do to earn a five-star review? And what were the circumstances around any negative reviews? How did you handle yourself in each situation? Do you have any tips to share?

YOUR PHOTOGRAPHIC TRIUMPHS. Did you switch to a new lens, use a different camera setting, or come up with a creative background? Did a new camera or innovative editing software change your life? What else have you done that could help your experienced Etsy colleagues as well as those who are just starting out?

YOUR PRODUCTION NIGHTMARES. Have you ever been in a production bind? Maybe you had too much inventory on hand, items that were never going to earn back their production expenses. Or maybe a gargantuan order caught you empty-handed. How did you handle the problem?

YOUR SEO BREAKTHROUGHS. Have you had a post go viral? Did you see a surge in activity after changing your item tags? When you experimented with planting certain keywords in your product descriptions, item titles, and profile, were the results a roaring success? How else has your SEO-oriented marketing driven traffic to your site?

PRICING THE SMART WAY

When you become a seller on Etsy, you open a business with effectively no overhead (that is, costs like rent, insurance, heating, and other expenses not directly involved in producing an item). You also gain the opportunity to reach an international pool of potential buyers.

But having no overhead is not the same thing as having no expenses. You'll still be paying for materials, shipping supplies, and shipping fees, for example. And, in addition to paying 20 cents for each item you list, you'll owe Etsy 3.5 percent of the sale price of every item you sell.

If 3.5 percent seems like a big cut, try putting it in perspective. The listing fee and Etsy's percentage represent a very small outlay for services that include marketing, advertising, and tools for driving traffic your way. You're not going to go broke paying your listing fees and Etsy's cut.

What will get you into trouble is a poor business model. To maximize your profits, you need to be ruthless about evaluating the business model you're using. This means continuously examining your production times, the organization of your supplies, how much inventory you have on hand, and the choices you're making about your supplies and your production space. And you have to make sure you're following best practices in the area of pricing.

In fact, the way you handle pricing is key to making sales on Etsy. A lower price doesn't always clinch a sale. In fact, prices that are too low eliminate the type of customer who assumes that a low price means poor quality. Prices that are too low are also the fast track to turning your business into a hobby. In addition, you will want any item's price to be high enough for you to lower it—for a sale, a coupon, or a wholesale or bulk order—without losing money on the item. Your lowest price still has to make you a profit.

But pricing through the roof is not a quick fix, either. Overpricing and an inflated sense of your product's worth will also interfere with sales. If your prices are higher than those of your competitors, on Etsy and beyond, you'll have to justify that difference in a way that motivates a potential buyer. In other words, you have to inspire customers' brand loyalty, which they may be willing to extend because of the personality and quality of your shop, for example, or because your shop offers a range of complementary items that offer the customer a one-stop-shopping experience.

Appropriate pricing, high or low, requires constant awareness of your competition's prices, dedication to reducing your costs without sacrificing the quality of your products, and an objective assessment of your brand's potential and of how you stack up against your competition.

You also have to figure out how many items of a particular kind you'll have to sell, and at what price, in order to net the amount you want after you've deducted your production and shipping costs:

- How long does it take you to produce this item?
- Could you produce it more efficiently?

- What hourly rate is acceptable to you as compensation for the time you spend producing, marketing, and shipping this item?
- Are you doing your production work, marketing, and shipping during normal business hours? Or are you producing, marketing, and shipping this item after hours because you have a day job?
- How much would you have to earn from sales of this item in order to quit your day job or go part-time and produce the item during normal business hours?

You also need to conduct a thorough evaluation of your production costs. Here are some tips to keep in mind for reducing costs and avoiding returns:

- **MAKE YOUR ITEM IN THE SHORTEST POSSIBLE AMOUNT OF TIME.** Can you skip or combine any steps? Can you produce any part of the item in bulk?
- **BUY AND USE SUPPLIES IN THE MOST COST-EFFECTIVE WAY.** Have you experimented with less expensive materials? Is there any part of the item that is not visible to the customer that you can find at a lower cost?
- **KEEP YOUR SPACE ORGANIZED.** This will streamline your production time.
- **ALWAYS HAVE ENOUGH SUPPLIES ON HAND.** This will save time in purchasing.
- **MAKE SURE YOU HAVE AMPLE INVENTORY, AND KNOW HOW MUCH YOU HAVE.** This will help you avoid last-minute assembly costs.

- **TEST YOUR SHIPPING SUPPLIES FOR DURABILITY.** This will help you prevent the cost of returns by reducing the risk of item damage during shipment.
- **TREAT YOUR CUSTOMERS WELL.** Be courteous, prompt, and reliable. This will help prevent returns while encouraging repeat business.

ACTION STEPS

☐ **ASSESS.** Make an assessment of your inventory, and analyze all your costs. These may include materials for your items, materials for your production line, shipping and packaging costs, and your labor. When figuring your labor, don't forget to include time spent in your work environment as well as the time you spend as an entrepreneur to market, brand, and promote your product, plus the time you devote as a business-person to handling customer relations and running your shop.

☐ **EVALUATE.** Take a look at your competition, and assess your prices in comparison.

☐ **ADJUST.** After evaluating the competition, make any necessary adjustments to your prices, and keep track of any differences in sales after a month of the new prices. Then adjust your prices again if you need to.

READY TO QUIT YOUR DAY JOB?

Once you come to see your Etsy shop as your primary source of income, it may be time to quit your day job. How do you make that decision? Start by considering your values regarding time, money, and quality of life:

- If you quit your day job, run your Etsy shop full-time for a while, and then decide to return to the workforce, how employable will you be?

- Does your day job cover your monthly expenses, or are you already on your own for medical insurance, taxes, retirement, and savings?

- How much do you need in savings to feel comfortable focusing all your energy and resources on your Etsy shop?

- How much stress does your day job contribute to your life?

- Does the thought of a full-time Etsy business fill you with happiness?

Consider quitting your day job when you reach whichever of the following milestones you feel most comfortable with:

- Your Etsy shop generates enough profit (as opposed to gross revenue) to cover your monthly expenses.

- Your Etsy shop generates enough profit to cover your monthly expenses and allow you to put money aside for taxes, retirement, and medical expenses.

- Your Etsy shop generates enough profit to cover your monthly expenses and allow you to put money aside for taxes, retirement, and medical expenses in addition to savings and an emergency fund.

MARKETING ON SOCIAL MEDIA

Think of social media as a free marketing tool. Remember, you want to be visible on the Internet and spread awareness of your brand. That means getting your brand in front of as many people as you can.

Heavy hitters like Facebook, Twitter, Tumblr, Instagram, and Pinterest have millions of users, and there's no reason why they can't also become your customers. Each of these sites has its own characteristic features and a particular culture, and you can learn to direct traffic from each of them to your Etsy page and your products.

The important thing to remember about any social media site is that people don't go there to shop. People are there to socialize, be entertained and amused, and maybe learn something new. But even though a site's users are not necessarily shopping, they're always open to finding something unexpected, and your product may be just the thing. The trick is to fit in.

- **POST A PHOTO OR VIDEO.** Give people something beautiful to look at: your product. Include a short description, and remember to link your photo or video to your Etsy shop.
- **POST A CURATED LIST OF ITEMS FROM YOUR OWN AND OTHERS' ETSY SHOPS.** Always remember how important it is to engage with the Etsy community and Etsy colleagues and teams. When your post of curated items drives traffic to your own and others' Etsy shops, every seller involved gets more page views, and the wide range of choices for

prospective customers enhances Etsy's reputation as a go-to shopping site. Besides, on a social media site where people are not primarily shopping, generosity and a soft-sell approach will strike the right tone.

- **OFFER A DEAL, A COUPON, OR A GIVEAWAY.** Such offers are all but guaranteed to bring new traffic to your Etsy shop. Not only that, people who already feel ahead of the game may very well buy something else when they visit your shop to redeem an offer.

- **INCLUDE SOMETHING SHAREABLE.** This can mean something funny, heartwarming, or newsworthy—anything that people immediately want to pass on to their Facebook friends or Twitter followers. Naturally, you'll relate this content to your product and include a link to your Etsy shop.

- **WRITE ABOUT YOURSELF.** Share what you've learned about patterns, fabrics, storage, or setting up a workspace. Build intimacy with your prospective customers by writing about creative blocks and breakthroughs. Tell people about someone who inspired you. Talk about the lessons you learned when experience was your only teacher.

PLATFORM	NUMBER OF USERS	PURPOSE	CHARACTERISTIC FEATURES
Facebook	1.3 billion	Social networking, photo sharing	Likes, status updates
Twitter	500 million	Social networking	140-character tweets
Tumblr	460 million	Social networking, microblogging	Multimedia content
Instagram	300 million	Social networking, mobile photo sharing, video sharing	Photographic filters
Pinterest	50 million	Photo sharing, business promotion, documentation of style trends	Pins

But before you post your first photo, video, list, status update, or tweet, you need to take three steps:

1. **SET UP AN ACCOUNT ON EACH OF THE SOCIAL MEDIA PLATFORMS YOU WANT TO USE.** Make sure that everything about your account has the same look and feel as your Etsy shop and communicates your brand across all the platforms where you've established a presence.

2. **CREATE ENOUGH CONTENT FOR SEVERAL MONTHS.** Gather photos of your products. Write short articles or blog posts about your products' features. Curate content specific to holidays and the seasons of the year.

3. **SET UP A MASTER CONTENT CALENDAR.** This calendar should cover at least six months. On what days of the week will you post, and on which platforms? How will you coordinate your posts across the different platforms?

ACTION STEPS

☐ **STREAMLINE.** Open your social media accounts, and streamline the images, fonts, colors, and messages on all accounts for a unified brand presentation.

☐ **PREPARE.** Gather images, write articles and blog posts, and generate other content in advance. Create a posting plan, and schedule your content across your various social media accounts at least six months in advance.

☐ **GENERATE.** Create more content around themes, holidays, seasons, and release of your new products.

PINTEREST MARKETING:
10 GO-TO TIPS

1. **PRICE IT.** Pinterest can drive customers directly to your Etsy shop, and pins with prices attached get more "likes" than pins without prices. People like to know what they are dealing with before clicking through, so take the risk, believe in your price, and go for it!

2. **KEYWORD IT.** Now that you know how to find the best keywords ever, make sure to include them in your Pinterest profile and pin descriptions so searches will find your products.

3. **"RICH PIN" IT.** Rich pins allow more room for description (which means that more keywords can be placed), and they automatically update prices and product availability.

4. **DISCOUNT IT.** Pinterest is filled with women looking for a sale. Adding the words *free*, *discount*, *deal*, and *save* will take you far in terms of generating interest.

5. **BOARD IT.** Title your pinboards with keywords like "*home décor*" and "*men sunglasses*" to connect with what buyers are shopping for.

6. **SHARE IT.** To build your visibility on Pinterest, add the Pin It button to images on your website or Facebook page. You can

even include the Pin It button in your e-mails. You can also offer the Pin It For Later link so people visiting your site or social media page can add your images to their Pinterest boards when they are ready.

7. <u>LINK IT.</u> On every one of your pins, include a link from Pinterest to your Etsy shop.

8. <u>PROMOTE IT.</u> Using e-mail, Twitter, or Facebook, let your audience know you have a Pinterest page.

9. <u>TREND IT.</u> Find popular pinboards, and pin there with the aim of garnering more followers and repins.

10. <u>THEME IT.</u> Create a theme, and pin accordingly. Holidays are a perfect theme to rally around and create a whole board on. Colors are another theme to experiment with—try a whole board of black and white, red, or rainbow hues. Be creative.

STRENGTHENING YOUR BRAND

Your brand is bigger than the particular items you sell. Your brand is the experience your shop promises.

It's all about customers' trust. When customers come to know that they can depend on you for a consistent experience—a look and feel that carries through in all your products as well as in your banner, your product descriptions, your photographs, the information in your profile, your presence on social media, and even the comments you leave at other sellers' Etsy shops—then you've done what's needed to win their loyalty to your brand.

To get a sense of what moves you, study the brands you love. Then take the following steps to strengthen your own brand:

- **WRITE A MISSION STATEMENT.** It should express what your brand stands for, what your company is about, and what you ultimately want to be remembered for. Start from this big picture of who you are as a company, and work from there.
- **HOME IN ON HOW ALL YOUR PRODUCTS WORK TOGETHER TO SUPPORT YOUR BRAND.** Are any of your products outdated? Do any need to be modified? Does anything have to go because it's irrelevant or contradictory to your mission statement? Do any products need to be added? Should you expand your product line to give your customers more versions of something they like? Carefully consider every product in your shop.

- **TAKE AN UNSENTIMENTAL LOOK AT YOUR IMAGES.** You can't afford to be attached to anything that doesn't work for your brand. Assess every image on your site, including your profile picture, your product photos, and your logo. Does anything stand out—and not in a good way? If so, remove and replace it now.
- **TURN A COLD EYE TO YOUR COPY.** Your copy, of course, is all the text associated with your shop. Does your copy say what you want it to say? Does it convey the essence of your brand? Does any of your language detract from your brand's message? Is there anything that doesn't fit? For example, if your brand is all about urban funk and cool, but your language is formal, then your copy is incompatible with your brand. If your photos are elegant and you want your brand to provide a top-drawer Tiffany experience, then you'll be sending a mixed message with laid-back copy. This kind of incongruity creates mistrust. It tells discerning customers who know what they want that your shop is not where they'll find it. After all, if you don't care enough to make your words compatible with your images, why wouldn't a prospective customer assume that you take a similarly sloppy approach to quality control?
- **ANALYZE AND STREAMLINE YOUR ETSY ENGAGEMENT STRATEGY.** What Etsy teams have you joined? What favorite shops and items have you listed in your profile? Do these publicly visible choices go beyond your personal tastes to reflect your brand? For example, you may be a big fan of

argyle socks and artisanal vinegar, but they have nothing to do with the handmade meditation benches in your shop, so don't show them as favorites on your Etsy site.

- **BE WILLING TO GROW YOUR BRAND.** If you become known for one aspect of your shop that takes off unexpectedly, don't stand in the way of paying customers' enthusiasm—even if their favorite product from your shop is not your favorite. If you started out as a shoe brand but find that your belts and accessories are your biggest sellers, honor what your customers are telling you—as long as it's working, which means as long as what your customers love is consistent with your brand. Never let your preconceptions about your brand become the enemy of your shop's success.

ACTION STEPS

- ☐ **RESEARCH.** Examine a brand you love, and note its color scheme, fonts, imagery, and product lines. Make a list of what you love most about this and other favorite brands.

- ☐ **INSPECT.** Double-check all representations of your brand, including your shop header, profile, images, and product descriptions, and impose cohesion. Also make sure your social media sites have a complementary look and feel.

MAKING CONNECTIONS

The Etsy community is what differentiates Etsy from the Amazon and eBay marketplaces. Etsy puts concentrated effort into facilitating a strong community ethos among sellers, buyers, and Etsy employees.

For an Etsy shop owner, making and maintaining connections in the Etsy community is key to getting noticed by shoppers and sellers alike—and you do want to be noticed by both cohorts, because each one has great influence. Each one creates curated lists, writes reviews and blog posts, and can celebrate your brand and your mission if the connection is there. In fact, there are many ways for you to raise your profile in the thriving Etsy community, and doing so can only strengthen your brand and elevate your sales.

TAP INTO ETSY TEAMS

We discussed Etsy teams at the beginning of this book (see Understanding Possibilities and Avoiding Pitfalls, page 10). A team, you will recall, is a group of Etsy sellers who have something in common. Maybe all the team's members are sellers of vintage vases, or maybe they're all living in New York.

Any teams you join are listed in your Etsy profile so prospective buyers can easily bounce between your various shops for an experience that is both more tailored and more comprehensive. And as your prospective customers browse, you and your team members will find that all your shops and brands receive greater exposure.

Another way to build mutually beneficial relationships with your fellow Etsy sellers is to curate a list of items from a variety of shops—being sure to include your own. After you publish your list, send a link to the sellers whose shops you've featured. They will probably want to promote your list, and that will drive traffic to your shop, too, since your items will be featured on your curated list as well.

You can also reach out to fellow shop owners by writing an article or a blog post featuring a group of related shops. This kind of free, unsolicited promotion creates something of a mutual-admiration society and portrays you as having confidence in your own shop and holding an expansive view of the Etsy community. It also positions you to benefit from reciprocal accolades in the future. Again, be sure to send a link to anyone whose shop you've featured in an article or blog post.

In addition, you can find out which Etsy shop owners are in your geographic area and suggest that you all participate in a community-building activity, such as attending the same trade show or flea market. The impact of face-to-face connection can strengthen your online community as you and your Etsy colleagues gain a lived and felt experience of one another. This is the type of team activity that really encourages mutual support, so do consider joining a team, featuring your Etsy colleagues on a curated list or in a blog post, and reaching out to Etsy colleagues in your vicinity.

COZY UP TO COMMUNITY TASTEMAKERS

As discussed earlier, Etsy Tastemakers are groups of enthusiasts who curate lists of their favorite items on Etsy. Often these groups have some kind of institutional affiliation, such as an academic or workplace connection or a shared association with a publication or a retail enterprise that is already an established brand. Tastemakers already know what they stand for, so when they curate a list of Etsy items, they are expressing their affinity for particular products and saying that these products help extend the Tastemakers' own brands.

Your goal as a shop owner should be to have your shop included in as many of these curated lists as you can. One way to do that is to make contact with Tastemakers and introduce them to your brand. Here are five steps toward that goal:

1. **CONDUCT SOME RESEARCH ON CURRENT TASTEMAKERS.** Make a list of those Tastemakers with whom you are familiar and who may match up well with your brand. Also explore lists curated by some Tastemakers with whom you are not familiar. When you find groups of unfamiliar Tastemakers who might be a good match for your brand, add them to your list of Tastemakers, too.

2. **REACH OUT TO BOTH SETS OF TASTEMAKERS.** Send an e-mail to introduce yourself, offer a bit of information about your story, and include photos of your product, perhaps a quote from a customer review, and your request to have your product considered as an addition to one of their curated lists.

3. **OFFER YOURSELF AS AN ASSET TO THESE TASTEMAKER COMMUNITIES.** You're making unsolicited contact, so present yourself as someone who knows about brands and is alerting them to something they want to know: the fact that your brand is a great candidate for the lists they have already curated. Express your admiration for these lists.

4. **SUGGEST A FEW ITEMS THEY MIGHT ADD IN ADDITION TO YOUR OWN.** Tastemakers are interested in growing their curated lists and impressing followers, so offer to promote their lists on your Etsy page, in articles, or in blog posts. Every brand wants popularity and more online traffic.

5. **TO MAKE A REAL IMPRESSION, SEND TASTEMAKERS A SAMPLE OF YOUR PRODUCT.** Tastemakers affect buyers' decisions about where to shop and what to buy, so make the effort to reach out and establish these connections.

ACTION STEPS

☐ **JOIN A TEAM.** Find a team on Etsy, make a connection, add them to your profile, and remain an active team member.

☐ **COMMENT ON A FORUM.** Read the Etsy blogs and forum chats, making at least one comment per week. Every comment can pique the interest of a new shopper and drive traffic your way.

☐ **REACH OUT TO TASTEMAKERS.** Investigate all the current Etsy Tastemakers, and identify any of their brands that relate to and complement what you have created. Reach out to these Tastemakers, and introduce them to your brand.

IMPROVING CUSTOMER SERVICE

Stellar customer service should your top priority. After you've created your products to the best of your ability and attracted customers to your shop, it is vital that you deliver an optimum shopping experience.

High-quality customer service includes presenting your products in an attractive way, responding to customers' inquiries and requests, and providing a smooth purchasing experience, which includes reliable shipping. Your customers have every right to expect a professional experience with you. The fact that Etsy shop owners are independent entrepreneurs does nothing to alter that expectation. Buyers want to experience all the positive things they have come to expect from an Amazon purchase or from shopping at the local mall.

Providing superior customer service is crucial. Customers are a source of repeat business as well as referrals. Etsy shoppers are often participants in the Etsy community, too. They pick their favorite shops, curate lists of favorite items, and write product reviews.

Every customer will have one of three types of shopping experiences with you:

1. A neutral experience

2. An amazing experience, one that potentially brings you hundreds more sales

3. An unpleasant experience, one that produces a negative review and dissuades other buyers from visiting your shop

In all your interactions with customers, remember that you are a business owner. There is no leeway for sloppiness or incompetence. Customers will not return if you slack off in any way.

PRESENT YOUR PRODUCTS ATTRACTIVELY

Your presentation of your product is an essential part of the customer's experience of your shop and your brand. Presentation begins with the customer's first view of a product photo and culminates in the customer's hands-on experience with the product itself.

That experience includes the customer's reaction to the external packaging provided by the third-party shipper (such as UPS or the US Postal Service) and the internal packaging that you provide. Everything, inside and out, should be clean, secure, and professional.

The interior presentation may include your business card, a charming sticker instead of tape to fasten the package, and such embellishments as tissue paper and ribbons. When you elevate your packaging from the ordinary to the extraordinary, you encourage the customer to have a positive association with your brand and your company.

RESPOND PROMPTLY TO CUSTOMERS' QUESTIONS AND REQUESTS

One of the most important connections you can make with customers comes from answering their questions and responding to their requests. You can answer a simple question with so much warmth that a customer immediately sees you as trustworthy and reliable. That's the kind of customer who comes back again and again.

A customer who makes an online inquiry is one step away from making a purchase. Don't make that customer wait for an answer. If you've ever waited in a store to ask a question while the salesperson took a phone call instead of attending to you, then you know how it feels to be pushed aside and treated as if you and your question don't matter. That's not the way you want to make your customers feel. Instead, let your prompt attention and your pleasant attitude say, "I am here for you. I can accommodate you. I want to make you comfortable with this purchase. Your satisfaction is my aim."

It's also important to respond to every type of communication from a customer. Thank your customer for a positive review left at your Etsy shop. And if the review is negative, rise above your anger or defensiveness. Simply express your thanks for the feedback, say that you take every review seriously, and promise to do better in the future. Your temperate response to the negative review may not change the unhappy customer's mind, but it will make a positive impression on future visitors who read it.

When it comes to customer satisfaction, leave nothing to chance. If a visitor to your shop makes an inquiry but then doesn't make a purchase, follow up. Ask pleasantly if there is anything you can do to answer a question or provide more information. And when a visitor does make a purchase and becomes your customer, keep in touch. Make announcements from time to time about your new products or send along some news about your shop.

You are cultivating a relationship with your customer. It's up to you to maintain and nurture that relationship.

MANAGE SHIPPING PROFESSIONALLY

A customer who has made an online purchase will be eagerly awaiting the package's arrival. That's why timely, reliable shipping is a crucial aspect of customer service.

Is your workspace organized well enough for you to manage your shipping operation efficiently? Do you have all the necessary packing materials on hand?

Remember also to take advantage of Etsy's shipping labels, which will save you many trips to the post office and allow you to send your packages worry-free around the world. Ensure safe and secure delivery by using protective padding, as appropriate, and a clear, neat labeling system.

And size does matter! A larger package seems more substantial, so it's better to pack a small item inside a large box than to stuff the item into the tiniest container you can get away with.

Speed matters, too, of course. Take extra precautions around major gift-giving holidays, when commercial delivery services and the US Postal Service tend to fall behind. Remember that every customer's purchase is tied to that customer's personal timeline, whether it involves an anniversary, a birthday, a wedding, or a remodeling or crafts project. If you promise a certain turnaround time, you have to deliver—literally.

DIVERSIFYING YOUR SHOP

It's all too easy to limit your shop and not even realize it. But think of some large national brand you admire, one that has a strong and secure brand identity, and ask yourself how it attracts so many different kinds of customers. Chances are this brand has learned to diversify.

If you decide to expand the range of customers your shop can attract, take care to maintain brand integrity. A solid brand comes first, so diversify within your brand.

Here are some ways to diversify and expand your shop's offerings:

- HAVE A RANGE OF PRICES. Is there something in your shop for every price range? A variety of prices, from the bargain bin to the top of the line, will attract more types of buyers.
- PRICE TO SELL. In addition to your fixed-price items, you can feature items that are priced specifically to sell. This is a widely used tactic for moving inventory. Choose an item, and dramatically drop its price. Some buyers' sole aim is to find a bargain, so you'll be appealing to a group of customers who may not have visited your shop before. Of course, you'll be introducing these customers to your full-priced items as well.
- CATER TO BOTH GENDERS. Try offering his-and-hers versions of your most popular items. And even if a particular item is specifically for women, you can adjust your branding and marketing to encourage men to buy the item for the women in their lives.

- **OFFER HOLIDAY-THEMED ITEMS.** There are plenty of major and minor holidays to choose from, and each of them can bring qualified traffic to your shop.
- **OFFER PRODUCTS IN SPECIAL CATEGORIES.** Can you maintain your brand while creating items that fall into particular categories, such as religious gifts, animal-themed items, items for infants and children, or bridal wear? By adding a few items that fall into widely searched categories, you may be able to reach a whole new spectrum of shoppers.
- **OFFER DIFFERENT VERSIONS OF CUSTOMERS' FAVORITE ITEMS.** Assess your best-selling items, and consider how you might create one or more variations.

ACTION STEPS

☐ **EVALUATE.** Check your current shop for diversification. Is your audience too limited in scope?

☐ **EXPAND.** Create one or more new product lines to reach more buyers. Broaden your price range. Consider adding items relevant to holidays, particular categories of items, and versions of shop favorites.

☐ **EXTEND.** You might also think about marketing to both genders and showcasing items that are priced to sell.

QUICK TIPS TO BOOST SALES

How can you stand out from the crowd and create a presence for yourself on Etsy? Boosting sales is not as hard as you think!

BE UNIQUE. Create a brand that means something to you. Have a voice, and use it. Stand for something. Let your shop be more than a place to purchase items. Make your shop an experience.

BE PROFESSIONAL. Make sure your photographs, models, backgrounds, banners, presentations, and communication all represent your company with 100 percent professionalism.

BE VISIBLE. Do your due diligence to make sure your keywords are relevant. Then place keywords and tags everywhere.

BE SMART. Utilize Etsy's tools to support your business. They were created by top talent with your success in mind.

BE SAVVY. Price to sell. Don't ignore the high rollers, and don't avoid shoppers looking for a steal. Reach them all.

BE ACTIVE. Post, pin, tweet, blog, snap, filter, upload, and engage. Social media platforms are hungry for your contribution, so make a splash.

BE PRESENT. Assess your progress in all areas of your company. How are you doing on innovation? Creativity? Reviews? Marketing? Production? Check in regularly with all aspects of your company to make sure all components are healthy and thriving.

BE CONNECTED. Etsy hosts a thriving community of shoppers, sellers, and administrators all eager to engage. Reach out, connect, and enjoy.

BE KIND. Customer service will make or break your shop. Make every customer feel special.

BE EXPANSIVE. Never limit yourself. Stretch. Diversify. There are many more buyers waiting to be invited to your shop. Find them, get to know them, and give them reasons to love what you have to offer.

SELLER'S CORNER

MICHELL

ETSY SHOP: GINGER SQUARED
ETSY.COM/SHOP/SHOPGINGERSQUARED

Michell is a California-based jewelry designer. Her Etsy shop, Ginger Squared, sells custom hand-stamped and engraved jewelry, including bracelets, necklaces, charms, and cuffs.

WHAT CHALLENGES HAVE YOU EXPERIENCED AS AN ETSY SHOP OWNER?

There are definitely challenges with competition, especially when it comes to making your items stand out among so many similar shops on Etsy. I can say as a vendor that the addition of non-handmade items here in the States has not been a favorite decision of mine or of many other vendors I know.

DO YOU HAVE ANY "MANAGING YOUR SHOP" TIPS?

The best pieces of advice I was given from another vendor were to update the titles of my products and use all the tags I can in order to generate more views. I can't promote using every tag enough!

Photos are also extremely important, and I think they can really make or break your interaction with new customers. I have noticed that having photos of my jewelry on models has made a big difference in how popular an item has been.

I am also continually trying to add new products and take out older ones that didn't seem to be popular.

Packaging is another really important part of an Etsy business. Presentation is key, and I am always impressed when I receive something that has cute and personal packaging.

HAVE YOU USED SOCIAL MEDIA TO REACH OUT TO NEW AND EXISTING CUSTOMERS?

Facebook was the place to start marketing a couple of years back, but it has not been a major player for a lot of vendors. Instagram is the place where I currently spend most of my time trying to reach new customers, and it has been a huge eye-opener. I had no idea that some people were able to run a shop strictly from their Instagram pages—and that it had such quick results!

DO YOU HAVE ANY TIPS FOR RETAINING RETURN CUSTOMERS?

I think good communication is key, so your customers really feel like you care about their needs. I try to check in and clarify with my customers as much as possible after reviewing orders since my shop has so much personalization to its pieces. Sending a quick thank-you note for an amazing review is another thing I have been trying to implement as well.

PART

3

BECOME AN
ETSY MASTER

I n this section of the book, you'll learn how to evaluate your success, identify your weaknesses, and surpass your original expectations by continuing to elevate your company. As a business owner, you need to be able to step back and view your Etsy shop as an independent entity that is separate from your ego, your attachments, and your emotional investment.

You must be willing to develop as a brand, as a company, and as a presence in the Etsy community. Celebrating your successes will let you expand on best practices and refine your most productive habits. Honestly assessing your weaknesses will let you discover strategies to improve. Sound business practice braids inspiration, smart effort, and good sense.

By the end of this book, you'll walk away with insider tips for getting your shop featured on Etsy and keeping it fresh and vital.

EVALUATING YOUR SUCCESS

There's always room for improvement, even when you're successful. Celebrate your achievements, but be ready to see things as they really are.

One way to do this is to engage in continuous self-assessment. Every time you evaluate your business, you have the opportunity to remedy your weaknesses and cultivate your strengths.

But without a healthy degree of separation between you and your shop, you probably won't make the best decisions, so you can also ask for feedback from customers, colleagues, and friends.

After you've made a sale, send the buyer a short survey. You may want to include a thank-you for completing the survey, such as a gift card or a coupon that can be redeemed toward the customer's next purchase.

When you ask friends and family members to weigh in, give them a short list of questions. You can share this list of questions with Etsy team members, too, and with your other Etsy colleagues. Include some who sell products different from yours, and invite them to do a peer review.

SURVEY YOUR BUYERS

- What attracted you to this product?
- Would you have been willing to pay more for this item?
- Was the purchase easy for you, or did you spend a lot of time thinking about it?

- Did the product meet your expectations when it arrived?
- Has anything been lacking in your experience of the product?
- What is your gender?
- What is your geographic location?

SURVEY YOUR FRIENDS, FAMILY, AND COLLEAGUES

YOUR BANNER

- What is your impression of my banner?
- When you look at my banner, what types of products do you think I sell?
- How does my banner make you feel? What type of audience do I seem to be catering to?

YOUR PROFILE

- What is your impression of my profile?
- Does my profile seem professional? Distant? Personal? Inviting? Too revealing?
- Is anything missing from my profile? If so, what do you wish I had included?

YOUR ITEMS

- Which of my items stand out the most?
- Do my photographs seem consistent?
- Do my items seem cohesive as a product line?

- Do you find any of my items particularly attractive or unattractive?
- When you look at photographs of my items, what kind of audience do you think I am catering to?

ASSESS YOURSELF

YOUR PRODUCT

- How much do you sell of each item?
- Do certain items sell much more than others? Can you pinpoint why these items outsell others in their category?
- Have you diversified your offerings? Are your products reaching as wide an audience as possible?
- Do you get many returns, exchanges, or reports of faulty merchandise?

YOUR CUSTOMER SERVICE

- Do your customers seem happy?
- Do they seem frustrated? Do they complain?
- How many of your customers return and make new purchases?
- How many write a review, positive or negative?
- How often do you acquire new customers?

YOUR PRESENCE ON SOCIAL MEDIA

- Are your posts relevant to the platform you're using?
- Are your posts viewed? Liked? Reposted?
- Are people clicking through from your posts to your Etsy shop?

- How many friends/followers/fans do you have?
- How many shares/likes are you getting?

YOUR VISIBILITY IN SEARCH RESULTS

- Where is your traffic coming from? Pinterest? Twitter? Facebook? Your blog?
- Which brings you more traffic: a blog post on your own website or a blog post on a third-party site?
- Have you used Etsy's Shop Stats utility to see which keywords are generating links to your products?
- Have you used 13 tags on Etsy for each of your products? Have you discovered the most popular keywords for your types of products? Have you inserted those keywords into product names, blog posts, and your profile?

ACTION STEPS

☐ **ASSESS YOUR STRENGTHS.** What areas are you successful in? What is effortless for you? Where are you most confident? Build on your success.

☐ **EVALUATE YOUR WEAKNESSES.** Where could you do better? Where are you weak? What is missing? What have you been avoiding? Where have you put in no effort at all?

☐ **GET FEEDBACK.** Ask for comments from customers, friends, family members, and colleagues.

☐ **CREATE NEW GOALS AND ACTION STEPS.** Use these to improve in your areas of weakness and to leverage your strengths for even greater success.

7 TIPS FOR KEEPING YOUR ETSY SHOP FRESH

1. **GIVE BUYERS A GLIMPSE BEHIND THE SCENES.** Create intimacy between you and potential customers by providing an up-to-date and visually interesting look at life in your shop. Photograph your production space and other elements of your shop in the most attractive way possible.

2. **CONTINUOUSLY ADD NEW PHOTOGRAPHS.** Most Etsy connoisseurs agree that photographs are as important as the items you are selling. Keeping your photographs current is essential to new business. Lure potential buyers with bright lighting, clear shots, and gorgeous backgrounds. Consider using professional software to edit photos. Beyond the words in your product descriptions, it's pictures that sell your items.

3. **OFFER A HIS-AND-HERS COMBO.** People love romance and "couple" gifts. Can you produce both a women's and a men's version of your top-selling item? Is there a complementary his-and-hers combination that could boost sales?

4. **INCORPORATE HOLIDAYS AND THEMES.** Surprise your buyers with a new line of products built around a holiday like Christmas or Valentine's Day, when they're primed to spend. Or create a theme based on springtime, for example, or on frequently searched keywords like "Bridal" or "Pet Accessories."

5. **MARK ITEMS DOWN.** Sales, bargains, and "deals of the week" help you spice it up. Keep the excitement of return visits alive. After all, if there is nothing new going on in your shop, why visit again? Let customers encounter the unexpected. When they think they're getting away with a great deal, the spending never stops.

6. **USE AN ATTENTION-GETTING BANNER.** Your banner is the first thing customers see when they land on your site. Make your banner effective. The look and feel should showcase the essence of your brand.

7. **TURN CUSTOMERS INTO VIPS.** Build brand loyalty by going out of your way to make customers feel special. Free items, discounts, and even the occasional "on the house" item will win you lifetime customers. For repeat buyers, send a handwritten note of appreciation with the shipment. Consider including bonus goodies in the delivery package.

MANAGING YOUR SUCCESS

To manage and build on your success as an Etsy shop owner, you need a strategy. That means being prepared to handle increased demand for your products without wasting valuable resources. It also means thinking about the long-term growth and health of your shop.

LEARN TO MANAGE YOUR INVENTORY

When you open an Etsy shop, start with a solid baseline amount of inventory. As sales come in, you'll need to adjust your inventory to customers' responses, replacing your items as you sell them and probably also expanding your product line.

As your shop grows, you'll learn the fine art of maintaining the right amount of inventory. Having too little on hand means a risk of coming up short when orders pour in and then disappointing customers, who hate to part with their money and then be told there will be a delay in delivering their goods. When you're low on inventory, you may be tempted to rush an order out, which can mean purchasing supplies at a higher rate and paying more for shipping. In addition, when you hit your suppliers with a sudden and unusually large order, you may create friction that affects your business relationship with them.

Here are some factors that often contribute to an unexpected increase in orders from customers:

- The rush around gift-giving holidays
- Your offer of products on sale or at a special discount
- A popular post about your shop on Etsy's *Seller Handbook*
- A popular article about your shop on a third-party website
- An increase in your activity on social media
- Your use of improved keywords and more relevant item tags

On the flip side of the question, having too much inventory on hand means you've paid to produce items that not only didn't sell but have also incurred expenses for storage (and maybe even for taxes). And storage itself involves a whole set of issues, such as protecting your unsold products from the harm that can be caused by heat, moisture, and insects.

To predict your orders accurately and increase your chances of having the right amount of inventory on hand, take a look at your sales from the previous year, and then estimate how much higher they're likely to be in the current year as a result of your adopting new and improved practices in marketing and promotion. The key is to *be prepared for success* so you're not undercutting your own best efforts.

DRAFT A FIVE-YEAR PLAN

If just getting through the day feels like all you can handle, then the thought of creating a five-year plan can seem overwhelming. But if you have no compass, you're flying blind.

Just as every redwood tree grows from a single seed—a tiny package that contains everything needed for the redwood sapling to become the giant of the forest—your imagination can hold big dreams that you'll achieve in small, measurable steps taken one at a time. Figuring out the direction and sequence of those steps is what long-term planning is all about.

To create your five-year plan, turn your imagination loose and let it lead you to a vision of your ultimate goal for your Etsy shop. Don't let doubts or insecurity creep in. Just think about what will make you happy. In five years, do you see your shop being featured on Etsy? Are you a team leader? Are buyers from major retailers beating a path to your shop's virtual door? Do you have the resources, storage, and capacity to fulfill big orders?

Now, on the basis of your ultimate goal, take these four steps:

1. Working backward, set an annual goal for each of the next five years.

2. Break each of your annual goals down into four quarterly milestones.

3. Break each of your quarterly milestones down into three monthly milestones.

4. Break each of your monthly milestones down into weekly action steps.

And now ask yourself these questions as you envision your Etsy shop in five years:

- How much revenue will it be reasonable for you to expect?
- How many hours a week will you want to be spending on the various aspects of running your business?
  - *Creating new products*
  - *Customer relations*
  - *Marketing and promotion*
  - *Accounting*
  - *Expanding your products and your sales venues*
- Will you want employees to handle any areas of running your business?
- What new skills will you need to learn?
  - *If you're new to SEO, will you need to take a class in online marketing?*
  - *Will you need to take a class in copywriting for better product descriptions?*
  - *Will you need to update your skills in photography?*
- What new or improved facilities or equipment will you need?
  - *Will you need a larger or better working environment?*
  - *Will you need better or different shipping supplies?*
  - *Will you need a better camera? Better lighting equipment? More sophisticated software for photo editing?*
  - *Will you need new software programs for help with invoicing and accounting?*

- What will you be doing to improve your visibility in search results?
  - *Will you need to enlarge your presence on social media? Increase the amount of shareable content you're posting? Create a well-planned content calendar?*
  - *Will you need to ramp up your engagement with the Etsy community? Join any new Etsy teams? Make more offline connections with potential customers at flea markets and trade shows or in boutiques?*
  - *Will you need to expand and/or diversify your products, perhaps by introducing theme-based items, appealing to seasonal shoppers, or building product lines around major and minor holidays?*

ACTION STEPS

☐ PREPARE. Be ready with expanded inventory when your product is in demand.

☐ DARE. Cultivate the self-confidence to look ahead and form a clear idea of what you want. Consider your long-term goals, and create a five-year plan.

☐ IMPROVE. Assess your strengths and weaknesses as a brand and a company, and resolve to try harder when you need to.

MAINTAINING A HEALTHY WORK-LIFE BALANCE

As your Etsy shop grows, so will the amount of time you need to put into it. Working for yourself can be liberating and intoxicating, but the line between work and life can blur or disappear when you haven't established clear times for clocking in and out.

To set up a good work-life balance, you need to know your values and figure out how to live by them every day. The time you spend on your company has to include production, branding, marketing, promotion, customer service, and accounting—and that's a lot. But you also need time to exercise, sleep, relax, have a social life, and attend to household routines and other obligations.

It is important to consider all your responsibilities, create a schedule, and stick to it. If you want to be your own boss, you need to be able to answer these questions in a way that satisfies you personally and allows you to meet your obligations to others as well as to your Etsy shop:

ARE YOU WORKING ALL THE TIME? Are you up all night? Do you work through meals? Do you work all weekend on your Etsy shop? Yes, there is a lot to manage. And, yes, you will reap the rewards. But balance is essential to your long-term health—and your company's.

EVEN WHEN YOU'RE NOT "OFFICIALLY" WORKING, DO YOU HAVE ONE FOOT IN YOUR ETSY SHOP? Do you say you're available for other activities when you're really on your computer and doing just one more thing

for your shop? It is important to set clear, intentional boundaries between time devoted to work and time earmarked for other activities.

WHEN ARE YOU MOST PRODUCTIVE? Capitalize on your natural rhythm of productivity, and recognize those times of day when you're working against your innate rhythm.

ARE OTHER OBLIGATIONS CREEPING INTO YOUR DESIGNATED WORK TIME? When you work for yourself, your work time is vulnerable to invasion by other activities and needs, whether your own or someone else's. You need to protect your workspace and your work schedule.

ARE YOU TRYING TO DO EVERYTHING AT ONCE? If so, stop now. Marketing, promotion on social media, customer relations, community outreach, product improvement, shipping, purchasing supplies, and accounting are all important, but the way to get all those bases covered is to create a weekly schedule with a slot for each of these important tasks. Your schedule should also include time for carrying out other duties and responsibilities as well as for maintaining your health and well-being.

GETTING FEATURED ON ETSY

Getting your shop featured on Etsy's home page should be your personal grail. Not only is this coveted recognition a feather in an Etsy shop owner's cap, it also gives a shop a big boost in visibility and opens the way to higher sales.

Here are some things you can do to position your shop as a strong competitor and bring your products to the attention of Etsy's administrators.

- HAVE A UNIQUE PRODUCT. Remember, Etsy was founded on the premise that allowing artisans with unique homemade products to mix it up with vintage collectors of one-of-a-kind items will offer customers something worth celebrating. And Etsy's administrators still have a soft spot for quirky innovators. Featured shops ultimately define Etsy as a brand, so Etsy is staking its reputation on your originality. Can your brand effectively represent the Etsy brand?

- HAVE A UNIQUE STORY. How did your shop come into being? How did you come up with the idea for your first line of products? Where do you get your materials? Does your brand involve an interesting partnership? Is there something unusual about your heritage or geographic location that plays a role in the products you create? Tell your story! Consider writing an autobiographical article or blog post about your journey, and then promote this material. Let Etsy know who you are—Etsy wants to know. The more distinctive you and your shop are, the more original Etsy becomes.

- **EMULATE THE BEST.** It's good business to acquaint yourself with what your Etsy competitors are doing. Find out who the featured shops' owners are and how long they've been on Etsy. Read their customer reviews, notice what Etsy teams they belong to, study their product lines, examine their photographs, research their item tags, and visit their social media pages to get a sense of their total online presence. Learn as much as you can from those who are already successful on Etsy.

- **BE IN THE KNOW.** What's popular on Etsy right now? Study Etsy's merchandising reports to find out what's happening seasonally, what the currently popular colors are, and what's trending on the site.

- **USE PROFESSIONAL PHOTOS.** Consider hiring a professional photographer to shoot images of your items. You can also explore software programs for photo editing to add filters, brighten colors, and fade backgrounds. Create six large, clear, crisp images of every item. The first photo shows the product as a whole and becomes your thumbnail for the item. The other five can include models, give a real-life context, or use an enticing background.

- **DRAMATICALLY INCREASE YOUR SALES.** When Etsy features a shop, the company is showing the greater Etsy community that Etsy knows what's popular with customers. The company wants to feature shops that have some buzz about them. One way to get your shop buzzing is to raise your sales volume to the point where it's obvious that you have your finger on the buyer's pulse and know how to deliver satisfaction. Significant increases in sales come from your integration of best practices regarding keywords, social media, photography, branding, marketing, and promotion.

- **BE THE BEST IN YOUR PRODUCT CLASS.** Etsy's administrators look at curated lists to get an idea of the shops and items that others have chosen to feature. It's in your best interests to get your shop onto as many curated lists as you can. Remember, Etsy teams create curated lists from items sold by their teammates, so join up! You can reach out to Etsy Tastemakers, too. Or take the initiative: Create your own curated list, and send it to the people you've featured. Maybe they'll return the favor. But even if they don't, you will have created a list that includes your product.

- **ACQUIRE THE LARGEST FOLLOWING.** Etsy will respond to your shop if you become unusually popular with people. This means developing large numbers of followers on your social media accounts, getting a big response to your articles and blog posts, attracting robust comments on your forum posts, and receiving reviews from your customers. Your following will increase as a function of your output and your willingness to engage.

- **CULTIVATE A COMMUNITY PRESENCE.** When Etsy features a shop on the site's home page, the company is deliberately giving that shop a marketing boost. Etsy wants to promote shops whose owners invest in the Etsy community, which means being active in the forums, offering tips in comments, and contributing well-thought-out advice to the *Seller Handbook*. Etsy loves team players, too, and when you join a team of compatible sellers, you show that you place value on what Etsy has to offer you.

- DEVELOP AN OFFLINE PRESENCE. You raise your odds of being featured on Etsy when you show up regularly at trade shows and flea markets. When you put time and energy into your brand at every level and in every possible venue, you raise your potential to make an impression on large numbers of customers, and your shop becomes stronger and easier to recognize.

SELLER'S CORNER

MISHA GURNANEE GUDIBANDA
AND AMIT GUDIBANDA

ETSY SHOP: SKY GOODIES
ETSY.COM/SHOP/SKYGOODIES

Misha Gurnanee Gudibanda and Amit Gudibanda are paper artists based in Mumbai, India. They've been actively selling paper gifts and printables on their Etsy shop, Sky Goodies, since Fall 2013.

WHAT HAVE YOU FOUND HELPFUL ABOUT
BEING A SELLER ON ETSY?

The exposure has been phenomenal. We have really enjoyed and learned from the beautiful work of Etsy artists—somehow the word *seller* does not do justice to the kind of quality you can find on Etsy. We have not yet had the opportunity to travel the world, but we have been able to discover amazing items from so many countries. People are also courteous and nice to do business with, both buyers and other sellers. This has helped us enjoy our work much more.

DO YOU HAVE ANY "SELLER SECRETS" TO SHARE?

It's not a secret, but we would just say do great work and give good customer service. I feel that a person on the other side of the globe is putting their faith in my product and paying for it up front; hence they are taking a risk. Answering their queries, being prompt in contacting them for any issue, is very important, to make them feel at ease.

WHAT ETSY TOOL DO YOU FIND MOST HELPFUL?

We use Stats all the time, and this is super helpful. One can deduce how traffic from different sources has different results: for example, a favorite or a purchase. Stats also help create material for social media. If traffic is coming from a particular blog, we can share that blog's page on our Facebook page. Plus, our Stats show seasons so beautifully.

DO YOU HAVE SHOP MAINTENANCE ADVICE?

We feel "cleaning up" or rearranging your shop regularly is important. Each time a sale happens on Etsy, the recently sold product comes to the front of the shop. Sometimes this can lead to very chaotic arrangements of items. We would recommend checking the shop appearance regularly, depending on frequency of sales.

CAN YOU OFFER ANY TIPS FOR INCREASING SEO RESULTS?

Just be thorough, use all 13 keywords, and try to think like the buyer. What would define your item, or what use would it fulfill? Your keywords should answer these questions.

DO YOU HAVE ANY TIPS FOR RETAINING RETURN CUSTOMERS?

Make the product so good that they will come back for more. Make the experience of interacting and buying as quick and easy as possible. We also offer discount coupons from time to time, and we inform our existing customers about the coupon codes. This makes them feel special, because sometimes these are not sales open for the public (the coupon code is not displayed on the shop).

RESOURCES

ETSY

Etsy app: www.etsy.com/apps
Etsy coupon codes: www.etsy.com/help/article/350
Etsy forums: www.etsy.com/forums
Etsy listing variations: www.etsy.com/help/article/3385
Etsy search: www.etsy.com/help/article/80
Etsy *Seller Handbook*: www.etsy.com/seller-handbook
Etsy shipping labels: www.etsy.com/help/article/3107
Etsy Shop Stats: www.etsy.com/help/article/541
Etsy Success newsletter: www.etsy.com/emails/success
Etsy Tastemakers: www.etsy.com/pages
Etsy teams: www.etsy.com/teams

PHOTO EDITING

Pixenate: www.pixenate.com

SEO ASSISTANCE

Google AdWords: www.google.com/adwords
Google Analytics: www.google.com/analytics
HubSpot Keyword Grader: www.hubspot.com/products/seo

SOCIAL MEDIA

Facebook: www.facebook.com
Pinterest: www.pinterest.com
Tumblr: www.tumblr.com
Twitter: www.twitter.com

INDEX